forgiveness

A Guide *for* Prayer

Dear Castro
Mr

Franisdiny Sinton
Thanks for your treat.

forgiveness

A Guide *for* Prayer

Jacqueline Syrup Bergan *and* Sister Marie Schwan

LOYOLA PRESS.
A JESUIT MINISTRY
Chicago

LOYOLA PRESS.
A JESUIT MINISTRY

3441 N. Ashland Avenue
Chicago, Illinois 60657
(800) 621-1008
www.loyolapress.com

The first edition of this book was published by Saint Mary's Press, (Winona MI: 1985). A revised and updated edition was published by The Word Among Press (Ijamsville, MD: 2004).

Unless otherwise noted, Scripture passages contained herein are from the New Revised Standard Version Bible: Catholic Edition, copyright © 1989, 1993, by the Division of Christian Education of the National Council of the Churches of Christ in the United States of America. Used by permission. All rights reserved.

Cover images, top: iStockphoto/pederk; bottom: Thinkstock/iStockphoto

Library of Congress Cataloging-in-Publication Data
Bergan, Jacqueline Syrup.
  Forgiveness : a guide for prayer / Jacqueline Syrup Bergan and Marie Schwan.
-- Rev. and updated ed.
     p. cm. -- (Take and receive series)
  Includes bibliographical references.
  ISBN-13: 978-0-8294-3612-9
  ISBN-10: 0-8294-3612-X
1. Forgiveness of sin--Biblical teaching--Prayers and devotions. 2. Catholic Church--Prayers and devotions. I. Schwan, Marie. II. Title.
  BS680.F64B47 2011
  234'.5--dc23
                                                         2011030771

Printed in United States of America
11 12 13 14 15 16 Versa 10 9 8 7 6 5 4 3 2 1

To my mother and father,
Amanda Martell Schwan and Jerome J. Schwan
—Marie

Lord my God,
when Your love spilled over into creation
You thought of me,

I am
    from love
    of love
    for love.

Let my heart, O God, always
    recognize,
    cherish,
    and enjoy your goodness in all of creation.

Direct all that is me toward your praise;
Teach me reverence for every person, all things.
Energize me in your service.

Lord God,
May nothing ever distract me from your love . . .
Neither health nor sickness
    wealth nor poverty
    honor nor dishonor
    long life nor short life.

May I never seek nor choose to be other
    than you intend or wish.
Amen.

Contents

Introduction

IF YOU ARE READING THIS page, you are holding the new edition of the second volume of the Take and Receive series, *Forgiveness*. It follows and builds upon the first volume, *Love*. Like the first volume, this book continues to open the treasure of the Spiritual Exercises of St. Ignatius of Loyola.

We are pleased that Loyola Press is republishing the series, continuing to make it available to people, and making it part of the repository of Ignatian Spirituality that is their mission.

Over the past twenty-five years, the series has served countless men and women, lay people and religious, Christians of every denomination. Remarkably, the content and approach—and the various exercises of the volume—have proven helpful. For this reason we have made minimal changes to the content for this fresh edition.

The dynamic of the Exercises is true to human experience. Once a person has experienced the incredible and personal love of God, he or she eventually becomes aware of the obstacle to that love: our sinfulness. As painful as this realization may be, it is also a gift as we enter into the deeper understanding that, though we are sinners, we are *loved sinners*, loved by our all-forgiving and merciful God.

This book takes on acute importance today as Christians are called to confront social sin and our own complicity in it. We live and breathe in a society in which the abuse of power is seen as a way to peace. We live in a time when injustice is too often a way of life, creating systemic sin: materialism, inequitable economic and political structures, worldwide fearfulness, commerce based on addiction, abusive labor practices, human trafficking, oppression of the poor, and the exploitation and wasteful disregard of the environment.

Because of the seriousness of this growing awareness, we heartily recommend that those who use this book have a spiritual companion who can offer wisdom and support.

The book, like the first week of the Spiritual Exercises, leads to an experience of the call of Christ and our response, a call to be members of the cosmic Christ and to promote the loving unity of all beings.

We have pledged ourselves to hold in prayer all those who make use of this book as well as all those who have been part of supporting both the writing and publishing of *Forgiveness*. With you we pray:

> *Let Israel rely on the Lord*
>   as much as the watchman on the dawn!
> For it is with God that mercy is to be found,
>   and a generous redemption;
> It is he who redeems Israel from all their sins.
>
> (Ps. 130:7–8)

Jacqueline Syrup Bergan   *Marie Schwan, CSJ*
Feast of the Assumption, 2011

Getting Started: How to Pray

Lord, teach us to pray.

LUKE 11:1

PRAYER IS OUR PERSONAL RESPONSE to God's presence. Just as Jesus was present to his first disciples, so God is present to each of us every day. Therefore, we can approach him reverently with a listening heart. He speaks first to us. In prayer, we acknowledge his presence and in gratitude respond to him in love. The focus is always on God and what he does. The following suggestions are offered as ways that will help us be attentive to God's word and to respond to it uniquely.

Daily Pattern of Prayer

For each period of prayer, use the following pattern:

Before Prayer—Preparation

Plan to spend at least twenty minutes to one hour in prayer daily. Although there is nothing "sacred" about sixty minutes, most people find that an hour better provides for quieting themselves and entering fully into the Scripture passage. To better prepare your heart and mind, take time the evening before to read the commentary as well as the Scripture passage for the following day. Just before falling asleep, recall the Scripture passage.

During Prayer—Structuring Your Time

As you begin your prayer time, quiet yourself; be still inside and out. Relax and breathe in and out, deeply and slowly. Repeat several times.

Realize that you are nothing without God and declare your dependence on him. Ask him for the grace you want and need. Then read and reflect on your chosen Scripture passage, using the appropriate form, such as meditation for poetic and nonstory passages or contemplation for stories or events. (See the section on the variety of ways to pray privately, page 3). Close the prayer period with a time of conversation with Jesus and his Father. Speak to God personally and listen attentively. Conclude with the Our Father.

After Prayer—Review

At the conclusion of the prayer period, take the time for review and reflection. The purpose of the review is to heighten your awareness of how God has been present to you during the prayer period. The review focuses primarily on what St. Ignatius described as the interior movements of consolation and desolation as they are revealed in your feelings of joy, peace, sadness, fear, ambivalence, anger, or any other emotion.

Often it is in the review that we become aware of how God has responded to our request for a particular grace or of what he may have said to us. Writing the review provides for personal accountability, and it is a precious record of our spiritual journey. To write the review is a step toward knowing ourselves as God sees us.

In the absence of a spiritual director or spiritual companion, the writing helps fill the need for evaluation and clarification. If you have a spiritual director, the written review offers an excellent means of preparing to share your prayer experience.

Keep a notebook or journal with you during prayer. After each prayer period, indicate the date and the Scripture passage that was the subject of your reflection. Then answer each of the following questions: Was there any word or phrase that particularly struck you? How did you feel? Were you peaceful? Loving? Trusting? Sad? Discouraged? What do these feelings say to you? How are you more aware of God's presence? Is there some point to which you should return during your next prayer period?

A Variety of Ways to Pray Privately

There are various forms of scriptural prayer. Different forms appeal to different people. Eventually, by trying various methods, we become adept at using approaches that are appropriate to particular passages and are in harmony with our personality and needs. This guide will make use of seven forms.

1. Meditation

In meditation, one approaches the Scripture passage as though it were a love letter. This approach is especially helpful in praying poetic passages.

To use this method, read the passage slowly, aloud or in a whisper, savoring the words and letting them wash over you. Stay with the words that especially catch your attention; absorb them the way the thirsty earth receives the rain. Keep repeating a word or phrase, aware of the feelings that are awakened in you as well as a sense of God's presence.

Read and reread the passage lovingly, as you would a letter from a dear friend, or as you would softly sing the chorus of a song.

2. Contemplation

In contemplation, we enter a life event or story passage of Scripture. We enter the passage by way of imagination, making use of all our senses. Theologians tell us that through contemplation we are able to "recall and be present at the mysteries of Christ's life" (13, p. 149).* The Spirit of Jesus, present within us through baptism, teaches us just as Jesus taught the apostles. The Spirit recalls and enlivens the particular mystery into which we enter through prayer. As in the Eucharist, the risen Jesus makes present the paschal mystery, in contemplation he brings forth the particular event we are contemplating and presents himself within that mystery. God allows us to imagine ourselves present in a specific Scripture passage, where we can encounter Jesus face-to-face.

To use this method, enter the story as if you were there. Watch what happens; listen to what is being said. Become part of the story, assuming the role of one of the persons. Then look at each of the individuals. What does he or she experience? To whom does each one speak? Ask yourself, "What difference does it make for my life, my family, for society, if I hear the message?"

---

* Numbers are keyed to the Bibliography, pp. 185–192

In the Gospel stories, be sure to talk with Jesus. *Be there* with him and for him. *Want him*; *hunger* for him. *Listen* to him. *Let him* be for you what he wants to be. *Respond to him.*

3. Centering Prayer

The Cistercian monk and writer M. Basil Pennington has noted, "In centering prayer we go beyond thought and image, beyond the senses and the rational mind to that center of our being where God is working a wonderful work" (25, p. 18)

Centering prayer is a very simple, pure form of prayer, frequently without words. It is a path toward contemplative prayer, an opening of our hearts to the Spirit dwelling within us. In centering prayer, we travel down into the deepest center of ourselves. It is the point of stillness within us where we most experience being created by a loving God who is breathing us into life.

To enter centering prayer requires that we recognize our dependence on God and surrender to his Spirit of love. *"Likewise the Spirit helps us in our weakness . . . that very Spirit intercedes with sighs too deep for words"* (Romans 8:26). The Spirit of Jesus within us cries out, *"Abba! Father!"* (Romans 8:15).

To use this method, sit quietly, comfortable and relaxed. Rest within your longing and desire for God. Move to the center within your deepest self. This movement can be facilitated by imagining yourself slowly descending in an elevator, walking down flights of stairs, descending a mountain, or going down into a deep pool of water.

In the stillness, become aware of God's presence. *"Be still, and know that I am God!"* (Psalm 46:10). Peacefully absorb his love.

4. Prayer Word

One means of centering prayer is the use of a prayer word. It can be a single word or a phrase. It can be a word from Scripture or one that arises spontaneously from within your heart. The word or phrase represents, for you, the fullness of God. Variations of the prayer word may include the name "Jesus" or what is known as the Jesus Prayer: "Lord, Jesus Christ, Son of God, have mercy on me, a sinner."

To use this method, repeat the word or phrase slowly to yourself in harmony with your breathing. For example, say the first part of the Jesus Prayer while inhaling, the second half while exhaling.

5. Meditative Reading

So I opened my mouth, and he gave me the scroll to eat. He said . . . eat this scroll that I give you and fill your stomach with it. Then I ate it; and in my mouth it was as sweet as honey.

EZEKIEL 3:2–3

One of the approaches to prayer is reflective reading of Scripture or other spiritual writings. Spiritual reading is always enriching to our life of prayer, but it is especially helpful in times when prayer is difficult or dry.

To use this method, read slowly, pausing periodically to allow the words and phrases to settle inside you. When a thought resonates deeply, stay with it, allowing the fullness of it to penetrate your being. Relish the word received. Respond authentically and spontaneously, as in a dialogue.

6. Journaling

The mystery was made known to me . . . as I wrote, . . . a reading of which will enable you to perceive my understanding of the mystery of Christ.

EPHESIANS 3:3–4

Journaling is meditative writing. When we place pen on paper, spirit and body cooperate to release our true selves. There is a difference between journaling and keeping a journal. To journal is to experience God's presence as we see ourselves in a new light and as fresh images rise to the surface from deep within. Journaling requires putting aside preconceived ideas and control.

Meditative writing is like writing a letter to one we love. We recall memories, clarify our convictions, and allow affections to well up within us. In writing, we may discover that emotions are intensified and prolonged.

Because of this, journaling can also serve in identifying and healing hidden feelings such as anger, fear, and resentment. When we write to God honestly, he can begin to heal past hurts or memories that have stayed with us for years. In addition, journaling can give us a deeper appreciation for the written word as we encounter it in Scripture.

Journaling in prayer can take various forms:

- Write a letter addressed to God.

- Write a conversation between yourself and someone else. The other person may be Jesus or another significant person; the dialogue can also be about an event, an experience, or a value. For example, you can give death, separation, or wisdom personal attributes and imagine each as a person with whom you can converse.

- Write an answer to a question, such as, "*What do you want me to do for you?*" (Mark 10:51) or "*Why are you weeping?*" (John 20:15).

- Allow Jesus or another person in Scripture to "speak" to you through the pen.

7. Repetition

I will remain quietly meditating upon the point in which I have found what I desire without any eagerness to go on till I have been satisfied.

ST. IGNATIUS OF LOYOLA (31, P. 110)

Repetition is the return to a previous period of prayer for the purpose of allowing the movements of God to deepen within the heart. Through repetitions, we fine-tune our sensitivities to God and to how he speaks in our prayer and in our life circumstances. The prayer of repetition teaches us to understand who we are in light of how God sees us and who God is revealing himself to be for us.

Repetition is a way of honoring God's word to us in the earlier prayer period. It is recalling and pondering an earlier conversation with one we love. It is as if we say to God, "Tell me that again; what did I hear you saying?" In this follow-up conversation or repetition, we open ourselves to a healing presence that often transforms whatever sadness and confusion we may have experienced the first time we prayed.

In repetitions, not only does the consolation (joy, warmth, peace) deepen, but the desolation (pain, sadness, confusion) frequently moves to a new level of understanding and acceptance within God's plan for us.

To use this method, select a period of prayer to repeat in which you have experienced a significant movement of joy, sadness, or confusion. You might also select a period in which nothing seemed to happen—perhaps because of your lack of readiness at the time.

To begin, recall the feelings of the first period of prayer. Use as a point of entry the scene, word, or feeling that was previously most significant. Allow the Spirit to direct the inner movements of your heart during this time of prayer.

Four Spiritual Practices and Helps

1. Examen of Consciousness

O Lord, you have searched me and known me.

PSALM 139:1

The examen of consciousness is the instrument by which we discover how God has been present to us and how we have responded to his presence through the day. St. Ignatius believed this practice was so important that, in the event it was impossible to have a formal prayer period, it would sustain one's vital link with God.

The examen of consciousness is not to be confused with an examination of conscience in which penitents are concerned with their failures. It is, rather, an exploration of how God is present within the events, circumstances, and feelings of our daily lives. What the review is to the prayer period, the examen is to our daily life. The daily discipline of an authentic practice of the examen brings about a balance that is essential for growth in relationship to God, to self, and to others. The method reflects the "dynamic movement of personal love: what we always want to say to a person whom we truly love in the order in which we want to say it. . . . Thank you . . . Help me . . . I love you . . . I'm sorry . . . Be with me" (10, pp. 34–35).

The following prayer is a suggested approach to the examen. The written response can be incorporated into the prayer journal:

- God, my Father, I am totally dependent on you. Everything is a gift from you. *All is gift*. I give you thanks and praise for the gifts of this day.

- Lord, I believe you work through and in time to reveal me to myself. Please give me an increased awareness of how you are guiding and shaping my life, as well as a more sensitive awareness of the obstacles I put in your way.

- You have been present in my life today. Be near, now, as I reflect on

  —your presence in the *events* of today

  —your presence in the *feelings* I experienced today

  —your *call* to me

  —my *response* to you

- Father, I ask your loving forgiveness and healing. The particular event of this day that I most want healed is . . .

- Filled with hope and a firm belief in your love and power, I entrust myself to your care and strongly affirm . . . (Claim

the gift you most desire, most need; believe that God
desires to give you that gift.)

2. Faith Sharing

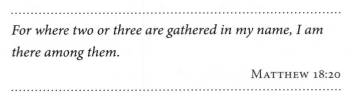

*For where two or three are gathered in my name, I am
there among them.*

MATTHEW 18:20

In the creation of community, it is essential that members communicate intimately with one another about the core issues of
their lives. For the Christian, this is faith sharing, and it is an
extension of daily solitary prayer.

A faith-sharing group, whether part of a parish, lay movement,
or diocesan program, is not a discussion group, sensitivity session,
or social gathering. Members do not come together to share and
receive intellectual or theological insights. Nor is the purpose of faith
sharing the accomplishment of some predetermined task. Instead,
the purpose is to listen and to be open to God as he continues to
reveal himself in the church community represented in the small
group that comes together in his name. The fruit of faith sharing is
the "building up" of the church, the body of Christ (Ephesians 4:12).

The approach of faith sharing is one of reading and reflecting together on the word of God. Faith sharing calls us to share
with one another, from deep within our hearts, what it means to
be a follower of Christ in our world today. To enter faith sharing
authentically is to know and love one another in Christ, whose
Spirit is the bonding force of community.

An image that faith-sharing groups may find helpful is that
of a pool into which pebbles are dropped. The group gathers in a

circle around a pool. Like a pebble being gently dropped into the water, each one offers a reflection—his or her "word" from God. In the shared silence, each offering is received. As the water ripples in concentric circles toward the outer reaches of the pool, so too this word enlarges and embraces, in love, each member of the circle.

Faith-sharing groups are usually made up of seven to ten members who gather at a prearranged time and place. One member designated as the leader calls the group to prayer and invites them to some moments of silence, during which they pray for the presence of the Holy Spirit. The leader gathers their silent prayer in an opening prayer, spontaneous or prepared.

One of the members reads a previously chosen Scripture passage on which participants have spent some time in solitary prayer. A period of silence follows each reading of the Scripture. Then the leader invites each person to share a word or phrase from the reading. Another member rereads the passage; this is followed by a time of silence.

The leader invites those members who desire to share how this passage personally affects them—whether, for example, it challenges, comforts, or inspires them.

Again the passage is read. Members are invited to offer their spontaneous prayers. Finally, the leader draws the time of faith sharing to a close with a prayer, a blessing, an Our Father, or a hymn. Before the group disbands, the passage for the following session is announced.

3. The Role of Imagination in Prayer

Imagination is our power of memory and recall, which makes it possible for us to enter the experience of the past and to create the future. Through images we are able to touch the center of who we are and to give life and expression to the innermost levels of our being.

The use of images is important to our development, both spiritually and psychologically. Images simultaneously reveal multiple levels of meaning and are therefore symbolic of a deeper reality. Through the structured use of active imagination, we release the hidden energy and potential to become the complete person that God has created us to be.

When active imagination is used in the context of prayer, and *with an attitude of faith,* we open ourselves to the power and mystery of God's transforming presence within us. Because Scripture is, for the most part, a collection of stories and rich in sensual imagery, the use of active imagination in praying Scripture is particularly enriching. When we rely on images as we read Scripture, we go beyond the truth of history to discover the truth of the mystery of God's creative word in our lives (12, p. 76).

4. Coping with Distractions

It is important not to become overly concerned or discouraged by distractions during prayer. Simply put them aside and return to your prayer material. If and when a distraction persists, it may be a call to attend prayerfully to the object of distraction. For example, it would not be surprising if an unresolved conflict continues to surface until you have dealt with it.

Section I

Called Out of Darkness

Week One, Day 1

Love Changes Everything

ROMANS 5:6–11

For while we were still weak, at the right time Christ died for the ungodly. Indeed, rarely will anyone die for a righteous person— though perhaps for a good person someone might actually dare to die. But God proves his love for us in that while we still were sinners Christ died for us. Much more surely then, now that we have been justified by his blood, will we be saved through him from the wrath of God. For if while we were enemies, we were reconciled to God through the death of his Son, much more surely, having been reconciled, will we be saved by his life. But more than that, we even boast in God through our Lord Jesus Christ, through whom we have now received reconciliation.

Commentary

GOD SO LOVED US THAT he sent his only son (John 3:16). And since then, nothing has been the same! Love changes everything. Love is the most powerful, the most energizing, and the most transforming force in the world.

The French Jesuit philosopher Pierre Teilhard de Chardin reminded us that "someday after mastering the winds, the waves, the tides and gravity, we shall harness for God the energies of love, and then for a second time in the history of the world, we will have discovered fire."

Our memories, like sparks of fire, are reservoirs of the power of the love we have experienced. When you recall the first moment you realized that you were loved by a particular person, you become present again at that moment in time. You are in touch again with the astonishment that he or she would love you. Somehow the love offered was too much to resist. When did you make the first response that led to surrender and that released and changed everything?

Love transforms us, and it does so not only in its initial surge of excitement, enjoyment, and new energy. It continues through the years to draw us toward wholeness—that is, to become all we are meant to be—loved, and loving. The miracle is that love continues, that it proves not to be a passing phase. Is anything so amazing as the fidelity of another loving us, one who continues to put self and interests aside for us?

If love between two people can have such an effect, the love that God extends to us in Jesus is even more astonishing and incomprehensible. The love toward which our human loving points is that which St. Paul describes as "God's love . . . poured into our hearts through the Holy Spirit that has been given to us" (Romans 5:5). However transforming and life giving a human love may be, it is transcended by God's love for us.

God's love remains a mystery. To speak of God's love as greater or better than human love is too simplistic. God is not a bigger or better parent, lover, or friend. Yet it is within our human experience that we can intuit the incomprehensible love of God. In our human loving, we are blind, tracing with tentative fingers the unseen features of God's face. In our fragile efforts to be consistent and faithful in loving one another, we catch a glimpse of the uniquely enduring quality of God's faithful love, a love made human for us in Jesus.

Through the death and resurrection of Jesus, the Spirit has been sent to us, and we are plunged into the fullness of a relationship with God and with one another. We need to approach the crucified Christ and see how much we are loved, to see there the kind of love that would prompt our willingness to give our life for someone we love. And we can, even within the limitations of human loving, imagine ourselves dying for our spouse, children, or friends. What seems impossible is to die for someone else who is unknown or unloved. And what seems even more impossible is that someone would do that for us.

This is precisely what Paul says God has done for us in Jesus. Jesus' death was the ultimate act of love for us. There is nothing more he could have done to show his love. And he did it voluntarily.

The love that shaped his death is the love that heals us, restores us, and transforms us. That love continues to be poured out for us through the presence of the risen Jesus—glorious, yet still bearing the wounds of his passion. He heals us in calling us to our own goodness, and he continues to do so.

Through his death and resurrection, we are summoned into the presence of the risen Jesus. We need only believe and surrender to that love—to say yes.

The wonder and beauty of our faith is that when we surrender our wounded selves, the power of the Resurrection is released in and through us. And we, as Christians—as Christ bearers—so live as to share with the world the love of our God as, daily, we lay down our own lives for one another. The Spirit of God's love, a spirit of trust that can empower us to live in joyful hope, has been poured into our hearts.

Suggested Approach to Prayer: Before the Crucified Christ

Daily Prayer Pattern (refer to pages 1 and 2).

I quiet myself and relax in the presence of God.

I declare my dependence on God.

Grace

I ask for the grace to experience the great love God has offered to me in and through Jesus.

Method: Meditation (refer to page 3)

I reread Romans 5:6–11 slowly, letting the words wash over me, savoring those that particularly attract me.

I go before the crucified Christ. I see Jesus hanging there, arms outstretched. I speak to him as friend to friend. I hear him speak to me of his love for me, in creating me, in being willing to die for me. I let the questions fill my heart:

> How have I through my life responded to the love of Christ?
>
> How am I responding now?
>
> To what does his love call me?

Closing

I pray the Our Father.

Review of Prayer

I write in my journal any responses I have had to the questions as well as any feelings I have experienced during this prayer period.

Part One

The Choice for Darkness

Week One, Day 2
The Rebellion of the Angels

2 PETER 2:1–22

But false prophets also arose among the people, just as there will be false teachers among you, who will secretly bring in destructive opinions. They will even deny the Master who bought them— bringing swift destruction on themselves. Even so, many will follow their licentious ways, and because of these teachers the way of truth will be maligned. And in their greed they will exploit you with deceptive words. Their condemnation, pronounced against them long ago, has not been idle, and their destruction is not asleep.

For if God did not spare the angels when they sinned, but cast them into hell and committed them to chains of deepest darkness to be kept until the judgment; and if he did not spare the ancient world, even though he saved Noah, a herald of righteousness, with seven others, when he brought a flood on a world of the ungodly; and if by turning the cities of Sodom and Gomorrah to ashes he condemned them to extinction and made them an example of what is coming to the ungodly; and if he rescued Lot, a righteous man greatly distressed by the licentiousness of the lawless (for that righteous man, living among them day after day, was tormented in his righteous soul by their lawless deeds that he saw and heard), then the Lord knows how to rescue the godly from trial, and to keep the unrighteous under punishment until the day of judgment—especially those who indulge their flesh in depraved lust, and who despise authority.

Bold and willful, they are not afraid to slander the glorious ones, whereas angels, though greater in might and power, do not bring against them a slanderous judgment from the Lord. These people, however, are like irrational animals, mere creatures of instinct, born to be caught and killed. They slander what they do not understand, and when those creatures are destroyed, they also will be destroyed, suffering the penalty for doing wrong. They count it a pleasure to revel in the daytime. They are blots and blemishes, reveling in their dissipation while they feast with you. They have eyes full of adultery, insatiable for sin. They entice unsteady souls. They have hearts trained in greed. Accursed children! They have left the straight road and have gone astray, following the road of Balaam son of Bosor, who loved the wages of doing wrong, but was rebuked for his own transgression; a speechless donkey spoke with a human voice and restrained the prophet's madness.

These are waterless springs and mists driven by a storm; for them the deepest darkness has been reserved. For they speak bombastic nonsense, and with licentious desires of the flesh they entice people who have just escaped from those who live in error. They promise them freedom, but they themselves are slaves of corruption; for people are slaves to whatever masters them. For if, after they have escaped the defilements of the world through the knowledge of our Lord and Savior Jesus Christ, they are again entangled in them and overpowered, the last state has become worse for them than the first. For it would have been better for them never to have known the way of righteousness than, after knowing it, to turn back from the holy commandment that was passed on to them. It has happened to them according to the true proverb, "The dog turns back to its own vomit," and, "The sow is washed only to wallow in the mud."

Commentary

THIS PASSAGE IS ONE OF many instances throughout Scripture giving evidence that, even before the creation of the earth, a spirit of evil had been unleashed in defiance of God. This idea is personified in the story of the angels' rebellion and fall.

The angels were the first and among the most magnificent of all of God's creations. They were under the rule and leadership of Lucifer, whose name meant "light bearer." The angels were free, pure spirits and had been given the gift of free will. God tested this freedom with an ultimate choice. Some of the angels failed, and they were cast into darkness. Lucifer—light bearer—henceforth became known as the Prince of Darkness.

We do not know exactly what the test was. St. Thomas of Aquinas suggests that it was one of pride, the motive of which was excellence. Created in the purity of grace, the angels were not prone to sin. Their rejection of God was an act of free choice. Some would suggest that they were shown a preview of God becoming human in the infant Jesus and were asked to worship him. Their sin, then, would have been one of refusal to submit to the seeming inferiority of Jesus. With that one act, the darkness enveloped them.

The story of the fallen angels provides us a way to grasp the deep-rootedness of our own collective sin. It is not enough for us to realize the pervasive darkness that overshadows our age. We need to go beyond that, to recognize that "sinfulness reaches down into the immense abyss of a sin occurring in a pure spirit" (59, p. 47). There is no immunity to sin. The fall of the angels is like a mirror in which we see reflected our own foolish and rebellious choices—not once, as with the angels, but many times.

In the second letter of Peter, the reference to the fall of the angels is made in the description of the subversive forces faced by the early church. False teachers, seductive leaders, and politically corrupt, influential people were making inroads among the members of the young Christian community. The corrupt leaders were motivated by greed and offered false promises of social freedom. Peter warns the people of impending punishment, using examples from the past. He presents as the ideal Noah and Lot who, while living in the midst of evil, stood firm and did not conform.

When the angels sinned, God did not spare them. Yet God is merciful to his people.

Suggested Approach to Prayer: Into a Mirror

Daily Prayer Pattern

I quiet myself and relax in the presence of God.
I declare my dependence on God.

Grace

I ask for the grace of feeling shame and confusion as I reflect on the effect of one sin of the angels, especially when I consider my own many selfish choices. ("Shame" should be interpreted as a conscious awareness of the disorder and selfishness that permeate my attitudes or behaviors.)

Method: I Prayerfully Reread the Commentary

I imagine myself looking into a mirror of imagination and memory. I will let the story of the fall of the angels unfold before me. In mind and heart, I mull over the incredibility—and the effects—of the single decision and rebellious action of the angels. I look at my own many choices and acts by which I have turned away from God's love.

Closing

I imagine Christ crucified. I speak to him, in my own words, of this great mystery. Through one sin of rejecting God's love, the angels were condemned. I, who have repeatedly rejected his love through sin, am allowed to continue to live and am given many second chances.

I close my prayer with the Our Father.

Review of Prayer

I write in my journal any feelings, experiences, or insights that have surfaced during this prayer period.

Week One, Day 3

The Choice: Living for Ourselves or for God

GENESIS 3:1–7

Now the serpent was more crafty than any other wild animal that the LORD God had made. He said to the woman, "Did God say, 'You shall not eat from any tree in the garden'?" The woman said to the serpent, "We may eat of the fruit of the trees in the garden; but God said, 'You shall not eat of the fruit of the tree that is in the middle of the garden, nor shall you touch it, or you shall die.'" But the serpent said to the woman, "You will not die; for God knows that when you eat of it your eyes will be opened, and you will be like God, knowing good and evil." So when the woman saw that the tree was good for food, and that it was a delight to the eyes, and that the tree was to be desired to make one wise, she took of its fruit and ate; and she also gave some to her husband, who was with her, and he ate. Then the eyes of both were opened, and they knew that they were naked; and they sewed fig leaves together and made loincloths for themselves.

Commentary

SOMETHING WENT WRONG WITH THE human family to which we belong. What went wrong is depicted for us in the story of Adam and Eve as it is found in Genesis 3:1–7. Like the actors in a play, Adam, Eve, and the serpent enter the stage. As we watch, listen, and are drawn into the story, we must confront our own situation. It is not that we journey backward into time but that we look within the depth of ourselves and see there our collective solidarity with the human family.

The stage is set in the Garden of Eden, in primitive blessedness. Adam and Eve dwell there within an innocent state of freedom. All their needs are met, and they are in intimate friendship with God, who walks with them each evening.

The one condition that God has given them is that they not eat of the tree of good and evil. The prohibition regarding this tree represents the danger of going beyond the bounds of their created beings, beyond God's intention for them. God did not place upon them this condition because he was jealous or threatened that they might compete with him. Rather, he knew that within each individual there exists a great drive to reach the full potential of one's physical and mental powers. So powerful is this drive that it threatens to deny our truer self, and thereby deny God.

The Lord's prohibition was an expression of, and protection for, the way in which he had designed the human heart to become completely fulfilled only in him. God knew that Adam and Eve could reach their full potential only by accepting themselves as created beings and by surrendering to his love. The common interpretation of the tree in terms of pleasure, possessions, and power are all contained within this pursuit of self, in the drive toward completeness. The ultimate choice is self or God.

Enter the serpent! The tempting question arises through creation itself in the form of the serpent, seen for centuries as a symbol of evil. For the Hebrew people, the serpent personified the dark powers of healing, sorcery, and limitless power (8, p. 45).

Eve and Adam were faced with the choice. So the woman "took of its fruit and ate; and she also gave some to her husband, who was with her, and he ate. Then the eyes of both were opened." The world they saw before them was not the world they had envisioned. It was, instead, a world of darkness. They attempted to hide from the presence of God. But in the cool of the evening, he inquired, "Where are you?"

They were filled with fear and shame. They blamed each other and the serpent.

The fall of the angels, the first of God's creations, had been reenacted in the first human beings. In the last scene of this act, Adam and Eve are expelled from the garden of their innocence.

Suggested Approach to Prayer

Daily Prayer Pattern
I quiet myself and relax in the presence of God.
I declare my dependence on God.

Grace
I ask for the grace of feeling shame and confusion as I reflect on the effects of the one sin of Adam and Eve, and I consider my own many selfish and sinful choices.

Method: Contemplation (refer to page 4)
I place myself in the garden with Adam and Eve. In my imagination, I enjoy the beauty and fragrance of the flowers, the sounds of the water, and the presence of the animals. I accompany Adam and Eve as they walk and talk with God. I continue to imagine the story in detail and follow it through to its completion: the

entrance of the serpent, the disobedience of Adam and Eve, and the consequences.

Closing

I imagine Christ crucified. I speak in my own words of how for one sin the angels were doomed, for one sin Adam and Eve were expelled from the garden. And I, who have so frequently chosen self in favor of God and yet have been spared—how is it that I am not in hell?

I close my prayer with the Our Father.

Review of Prayer

I write in my journal any interior feelings, experiences, or insights that have surfaced during this prayer period.

Week One, Day 4

The Ratification of Sin

....

ROMANS 5:12–21

Therefore, just as sin came into the world through one man, and death came through sin, and so death spread to all because all have sinned—sin was indeed in the world before the law, but sin is not reckoned when there is no law. Yet death exercised dominion from Adam to Moses, even over those whose sins were not like the transgression of Adam, who is a type of the one who was to come.

But the free gift is not like the trespass. For if the many died through the one man's trespass, much more surely have the grace of God and the free gift in the grace of the one man, Jesus Christ, abounded for the many. And the free gift is not like the effect of the one man's sin. For the judgment following one trespass brought condemnation, but the free gift following many trespasses brings justification. If, because of the one man's trespass, death exercised dominion through that one, much more surely will those who receive the abundance of grace and the free gift of righteousness exercise dominion in life through the one man, Jesus Christ.

Therefore just as one man's trespass led to condemnation for all, so one man's act of righteousness leads to justification and life for all. For just as by the one man's disobedience the many were made sinners, so by the one man's obedience the many will be made righteous. But law came in, with the result that the trespass multiplied; but where sin increased, grace abounded all the more, so that, just as sin exercised dominion in death, so grace might also exercise dominion through justification leading to eternal life through Jesus Christ our Lord.

Commentary

ADAM SINNED—ONE PERSON, ONE SIN. Darkness and pain followed. Darkness and sin encircled the earth; no one has escaped its countless tentacles. It has spread into entire families, into the very earth itself. Through one act, sin entered the world and began to trace its path through history. No person, no social structure, sector, or institution, has been immune from its infectious presence.

Each of us, in this historical, collective dimension, sees ourself in Adam and Eve, and the penance of this original sin is visited on each of us. The past did not occur apart from the present. Our present reality is held within our past.

In every act of sin that is committed, the original sin of Adam and Eve is ratified (59, p. 49). Darkness precipitates darkness: in the breakdown of family with Cain and Abel (Genesis 4:1–16), then and now; in the breakdown of communication at Babel (Genesis 11:1–9), then and now; in the flood of wickedness (Genesis 6—8), then and now.

Into this darkness, Jesus comes. "For as all die in Adam, so all will be made alive in Christ" (1 Corinthians 15:22). Through a total surrender to God, Jesus reversed the choice of Adam. In Jesus, Adam's choice has been annulled.

St. Paul draws a parallel between Adam and Christ. It is not, however, as if they are equal counterforces. Where death does abound, there does life more abound (Romans 5:21). Good far outweighs evil, and in Jesus the death and destruction of sin are overturned.

Suggested Approach to Prayer

Daily Prayer Pattern
I quiet myself and relax in the presence of God.
I declare my dependence on God.

Grace
I ask for the grace of feeling shame and confusion as I consider the effects of sin.

Method
I carefully consider this passage of Paul and the commentary, with an awareness of the widespread destructiveness of sin in our world. I consider, If one act of sin was such a strong catalyst for so much evil in the world, what about my own many sins?

Closing
I go before the crucified Christ and reflect about this mystery of sin and speak to Christ of whatever surfaces in my mind and heart.

I close my prayer with the *Our Father.*

Review of Prayer
I write in my journal any feelings, experiences, or insights that have come to my awareness during this prayer period.

Week One, Day 5

One Person's Fall

....

LUKE 16:19–31

"There was a rich man who was dressed in purple and fine linen and who feasted sumptuously every day. And at his gate lay a poor man named Lazarus, covered with sores, who longed to satisfy his hunger with what fell from the rich man's table; even the dogs would come and lick his sores. The poor man died and was carried away by the angels to be with Abraham. The rich man also died and was buried.

"In Hades, where he was being tormented, he looked up and saw Abraham far away with Lazarus by his side. He called out, 'Father Abraham, have mercy on me, and send Lazarus to dip the tip of his finger in water and cool my tongue; for I am in agony in these flames.' But Abraham said, 'Child, remember that during your lifetime you received your good things, and Lazarus in like manner evil things; but now he is comforted here, and you are in agony. Besides all this, between you and us a great chasm has been fixed, so that those who might want to pass from here to you cannot do so, and no one can cross from there to us.'

"He said, 'Then, father, I beg you to send him to my father's house—for I have five brothers—that he may warn them, so that they will not also come into this place of torment.' Abraham replied, 'They have Moses and the prophets; they should listen to them.' He said, 'No, father Abraham; but if someone goes to them from the dead, they will repent.' He said to him, 'If they do not listen to Moses and the prophets, neither will they be convinced even if someone rises from the dead.'"

Commentary

THE SIN OF THE RICH man was not that he was rich.

He *was* rich! He was rich materially. He dressed in fine linen and royal purple, the dye of which was obtained from exotic shellfish available only to the very wealthy. The color itself was a status symbol. Every day was a gourmet feast! In a country where meat was scarce, he ate it daily.

Dives—as he is usually called—was rich also in privilege and status. He was "clearly a Sadducee, not only because of his social standing, but because, as the story shows, he had no belief in an afterlife, in spite of the fact that he and his brother professed obedience to the teaching of Moses and the prophets" (16, p. 191). As a Sadducee, he was a member of the established religion. Membership gave him power and influence, along with the assumption that he was righteous and above reproach.

As someone who did not believe in life after death, Dives ironically discovers himself in acute suffering, cut off from life and condemned to eternal loss. He looks over the abyss that separates the damned from those who have been delivered into the presence of God. There he sees Lazarus welcomed and enfolded in the love of the God of Abraham. For the first time, the rich man recognizes and calls Lazarus by name. Yet even in these circumstances, the rich man treats Lazarus as his servant.

The sin of the rich man was not the fact of his wealth or status. It was not that he was openly or deliberately cruel. He did not, after all, remove Lazarus from his gate. He did not necessarily forbid him the scraps. He simply did not notice him, and that was his sin! Lazarus had become for the rich man an inevitable part of the social structure, always present, yet always unseen.

Luke (1:52) recounts Jesus' telling of this parable to continue his theme of exaltation of the lowly and the putting down of the mighty. Yet the story is more than a simple reversal of external circumstances. It is more than a story illustrating the reward of poverty and the punishment of the wealthy. It is a warning! It is a warning to those who claim to be believers, hearing God's word in Scripture and worship, but who do not bring their daily lives into accord with God's word.

The Jews believed that landowners were tenants of Yahweh (Leviticus 25:23) who paid taxes through alms to the poor, who were considered Yahweh's representatives. The rich man's blind indifference to Lazarus was a rejection not only of God's word but also of God. This was the sin of the rich man.

For the rich man, for his brothers, and for us, there are two failures, which belong together: "Where the mind is closed to the revelation of God, the heart is closed to the demands of compassion" (16, p. 192).

Suggested Approach to Prayer

Daily Prayer Pattern
I quiet myself and relax in the presence of God.
I declare my dependence on God.

Grace

I ask for the grace of feeling shame and confusion as I consider the effects of sin, and of feeling amazement before the goodness and mercy of God in preserving me from hell.

Method: Contemplation

I assume the role of the rich man and imagine myself wearing beautiful robes and feasting sumptuously. I see myself being unaware of people around me who are suffering. I imagine myself, in great detail, being in hell. I see my shock, confusion, and futile cry for release. I am aware of the images and conversations that are occurring.

Closing

I go before the crucified Christ and, considering my own sinfulness and lack of awareness, ask, "Why have I been preserved from the ultimate effect of my own sinfulness?"

I close my prayer with the Our Father.

Review of Prayer

I write in my journal any feelings, experiences, or insights that have surfaced during this prayer period.

Week One, Day 6

Repetition

Suggested Approach to Prayer

Daily Prayer Pattern

I quiet myself and relax in the presence of God.
I declare my dependence on God.

Grace

I ask for the grace of feeling deep confusion and sorrow as I consider the effects of even one sin.

Method: It will be particularly helpful to read "Repetition" on page 8.

In preparation, I review my prayer by reading my journal from the past week. I select for my repetition the period of prayer in which I was deeply moved, either by joy or by sadness. I proceed in the manner I did originally, focusing on the scene, word, or feeling that was significant.

Review of Prayer

I write in my journal any feelings, experiences, or insights that have come to my awareness during this prayer period.

Part Two

The Consequences of Sin

Week Two, Day 1

A Warning from History

··

EZEKIEL 16:1–22, 59–63

The word of the LORD came to me: Mortal, make known to Jerusalem her abominations, and say, Thus says the Lord GOD to Jerusalem: Your origin and your birth were in the land of the Canaanites; your father was an Amorite, and your mother a Hittite. As for your birth, on the day you were born your navel cord was not cut, nor were you washed with water to cleanse you, nor rubbed with salt, nor wrapped in cloths. No eye pitied you, to do any of these things for you out of compassion for you; but you were thrown out in the open field, for you were abhorred on the day you were born.

I passed by you, and saw you flailing about in your blood. As you lay in your blood, I said to you, "Live! and grow up like a plant of the field." You grew up and became tall and arrived at full womanhood; your breasts were formed, and your hair had grown; yet you were naked and bare.

I passed by you again and looked on you; you were at the age for love. I spread the edge of my cloak over you, and covered your nakedness: I pledged myself to you and entered into a covenant with you, says the Lord GOD, and you became mine. Then I bathed you with water and washed off the blood from you, and anointed you with oil. I clothed you with embroidered cloth and with sandals of fine leather; I bound you in fine linen and covered you with rich fabric. I adorned you with ornaments: I put bracelets on your arms, a chain on your neck, a ring on your nose, earrings in your ears, and a beautiful crown upon your head. You were adorned with gold and silver, while your clothing was of fine linen, rich fabric, and embroidered cloth. You had choice flour and honey and oil for food. You grew exceedingly beautiful, fit to be a queen. Your fame spread among the nations on account of your beauty, for it was perfect because of my splendor that I had bestowed on you, says the Lord GOD.

But you trusted in your beauty, and played the whore because of your fame, and lavished your whorings on any passer-by. You took some of your garments, and made for yourself colorful shrines, and on them played the whore; nothing like this has ever been or ever shall be. You also took your beautiful jewels of my gold and my silver that I had given you, and made for yourself male images, and with them played the whore; and you took your embroidered garments to cover them, and set my oil and my incense before them. Also my bread that I gave you—I fed you with choice flour and oil and honey—you set it before them as a pleasing odor; and so it was, says the Lord GOD. You took your sons and your daughters, whom you had borne to me, and these you sacrificed to them to be devoured. As if your whorings were not enough! You slaughtered my children and delivered them up as an offering to them. And in all your abominations and your whorings you did not remember the days of your youth, when you were naked and bare, flailing about in your blood. . . .

Yes, thus says the Lord GOD: I will deal with you as you have done, you who have despised the oath, breaking the covenant; yet I will remember my covenant with you in the days of your youth, and I will establish with you an everlasting covenant. Then you will remember your ways, and be ashamed when I take your sisters, both your elder and your younger, and give them to you as daughters, but not on account of my covenant with you. I will establish my covenant with you, and you shall know that I am the LORD, in order that you may remember and be confounded, and never open your mouth again because of your shame, when I forgive you all that you have done, says the Lord GOD.

Commentary

EZEKIEL'S LONG AND DRAMATIC ORACLE expresses his grief and abhorrence of sin, especially in the light of God's goodness. The lurid images and strong language, not generally found in Scripture, may be offensive on first reading.

This oracle is a prophetic warning. The warning takes the form of a story about the life of an abandoned child who, after having been found and cared for, rejected love and adopted a life of prostitution. Though the typical folktale of his time focused on the foundling as a hero, Ezekiel focused his story on the faithfulness of God in the face of the unfaithfulness of the foundling. Although the foundling-as-hero is always very appealing, Ezekiel uses the story like a two-edged sword to cut through and expose the reality and treachery of sin.

The story is an allegory of the history of the chosen people and their relationship with God. A parallel is drawn between the life of the prostitute and the history of the Israelite people. Like the beginnings of the life of the foundling, Israel's beginnings were also in the wilderness of Egypt. In God's "passing," Israel, like the child, grew in stature and beauty.

At the point of readiness, God claimed the young woman as his own. Israel too was chosen, and the relationship with God was like that of a marriage covenant. Not unlike the prostitute's rejection of love, Israel's history is marred by idolatry and infidelity. The chosen people made alliances with foreign kings, adopting their cultic worship of foreign gods. They even went so far as to practice human sacrifice.

As we read the passage, we are overwhelmed with the sense of the malignant, destructive character of sin. Sin perpetuates itself and feeds off others. It releases an alienating force of such strength that it isolates us from ourselves and from God. This is the anguish of Ezekiel as he ponders Israel's history of infidelity.

Ezekiel's intention is to move the prostitute toward a sense of shame and confusion. He calls on her to remember God's goodness to her and how faithful God has always been. Only in the memory of God's overwhelming love for her will she plumb the depths of her shame, be filled with sorrow for her sin, and be reconciled.

For the prostitute, for Israel, and for us, "the shame and disgrace over the past bespeaks the new impressionable, contrite heart that will animate the future" (33, p. 306).

Suggested Approach to Prayer

Daily Prayer Pattern
I quiet myself and relax in the presence of God.
I declare my dependence on God.

Grace
I ask for the grace of sorrow for sin.

Method: I read the passage from Ezekiel and the commentary carefully.
As the story and its meaning become clear, I will be aware of my feelings—my repulsions, anxieties, or other emotions. I will ask myself the following questions:

Can I, in any way, identify with the child—abandoned and uncared for?

Can I identify with the prostitute?

What questions surface within me?

Closing

I speak with Christ on the cross. I share with him whatever I have experienced through Ezekiel's passage.

I close my prayer with the Our Father.

Review of Prayer

I write in my journal my responses to the questions posed above.

Week Two, Day 2

Remembering

Reread Ezekiel 16:1–22, 59–63.

Commentary

IN A TIME WHEN ONLY a few people knew how to read, the early Israelites were almost totally dependent on memory. Repeatedly in the Old Testament, we find them being instructed to remember. "Remember the sabbath day, and keep it holy" (Exodus 20:8); "remember the wonderful works he has done" (Psalm 105:5).

The first five books of the Bible are called the Torah—meaning "law"—and contain the early history and stories that constitute the memory of the Hebrew people. Although there were many requirements in the Torah specifying how they were to regulate their lives, the essential, underlying *law* was that the people were never to forget God's goodness to them. They were to recall all the events and circumstances of their common history, in which Yahweh revealed his love. They were to celebrate his presence—past, present, and future.

At the heart of their worship was the remembrance of God's deed, their affirmation of his presence among them, and their trust in the new thing he would create among them. "From this time forward I make you hear new things, hidden things that you have not known. They are created now, not long ago" (Isaiah 48:6–7; see also Revelation 21:5).

Memory endowed the Hebrew people—and endows us—with a sense of rootedness, identity, and direction. To prayerfully remember is to cooperate with God in the "re-membering" of ourselves. It is to actively engage with the Spirit in uniting those fragmented areas of ourselves that have been split off and alienated through sin.

As we recall a particular event or circumstance in which we experienced God's love sustaining and directing us, two things occur: there is a deepening awareness of his faithfulness, and in the recalling, we open ourselves, mysteriously, to receive again the grace of that event, this time in greater measure and with a deeper level of healing. *"Remember and be confounded, and never open your mouth again because of your shame"* (Ezekiel 16:63).

Suggested Approach to Prayer

Daily Prayer Pattern

I quiet myself and relax in the presence of God.
I declare my dependence on God.

Grace

I ask for the gift of sorrow for sin.

Method

I walk through my life, remembering places I loved, and events, activities, work, and significant people. I recall God's expressions of love and how I have exploited, misused, or rejected that love:

Examples of God's Love	Ways I Rejected God's Love
As a child:	
As an adolescent:	
20–30:	
30–40:	
40–50:	
50 and over:	

(You may find it helpful to write this exercise in your journal.)

Closing

I see Christ on the cross. I thank him for his compassion toward me throughout my life. I thank him that he has sustained me to this point.

I close with the Our Father.

Review of Prayer

I write in my journal any new awareness that came to me during this prayer exercise.

Week Two, Day 3
Remembering, Part 2

Reread Ezekiel 16:1–22, 59–63.

Commentary

REREAD THE PASSAGE AND REVIEW whatever journaling you have done in the past two days of prayer.

Suggested Approach to Prayer

Daily Prayer Pattern

I quiet myself and relax in the presence of God.
I declare my dependence on God.

Grace

I ask for shame and confusion because of my sinfulness.

Method

I return to the prayer of the previous day: my own history of grace and sin, of God's love and my own rejection. As I review my history of sin, I focus my attention on whichever particular sin event God allows to surface most prominently. I prayerfully place myself in the situation of that event. I recall in detail all the specific aspects—the place, the people, the words, the thoughts, and the feelings.

I consider the consequences of this sin:

What has occurred as a result?

How has it damaged relationships?

How has it limited possibilities for myself and others?

What suffering has come about through my sin? Who has wept?

How has it reinforced and contributed to the evil that I see in the world?

Closing

I see Christ on the cross. I speak to him from the depths of my awareness. I thank him for not deserting me in my times of sin and brokenness.

Review of Prayer

I write in my journal my responses to the questions posed for this day.

Week Two, Day 4

You Are the One

....

2 SAMUEL 11:1–21, 27; 12:1, 7–10, 13–25

In the spring of the year, the time when kings go out to battle, David sent Joab with his officers and all Israel with him; they ravaged the Ammonites, and besieged Rabbah. But David remained at Jerusalem.

It happened, late one afternoon, when David rose from his couch and was walking about on the roof of the king's house, that he saw from the roof a woman bathing; the woman was very beautiful. David sent someone to inquire about the woman. It was reported, "This is Bathsheba daughter of Eliam, the wife of Uriah the Hittite." So David sent messengers to get her, and she came to him, and he lay with her. (Now she was purifying herself after her period.) Then she returned to her house. The woman conceived; and she sent and told David, "I am pregnant."

So David sent word to Joab, "Send me Uriah the Hittite." And Joab sent Uriah to David. When Uriah came to him, David asked how Joab and the people fared, and how the war was going. Then David said to Uriah, "Go down to your house, and wash your feet." Uriah went out of the king's house, and there followed him a present from the king. But Uriah slept at the entrance of the king's house with all the servants of his lord, and did not go down to his house. When they told David, "Uriah did not go down to his house," David said to Uriah, "You have just come from a journey. Why did you not go down to your house?" Uriah said to David, "The ark and Israel and Judah remain in booths; and my lord Joab and the servants of my lord are camping in the open field; shall I then go to my house, to eat and to drink, and to lie with my wife? As you live, and as your soul lives, I will not do such a thing." Then David said to Uriah, "Remain here today also, and tomorrow I will send you back." So Uriah remained in Jerusalem that day. On the next day, David invited him to eat and drink in his presence and made him drunk; and in the evening he went out to lie on his couch with the servants of his lord, but he did not go down to his house.

In the morning David wrote a letter to Joab, and sent it by the hand of Uriah. In the letter he wrote, "Set Uriah in the forefront of the hardest fighting, and then draw back from him, so that he may be struck down and die." As Joab was besieging the city, he assigned Uriah to the place where he knew there were valiant warriors. The men of the city came out and fought with Joab; and some of the servants of David among the people fell. Uriah the Hittite was killed as well. Then Joab sent and told David all the news about the fighting; and he instructed the messenger, "When you have finished telling the king all the news about the fighting, then, if the king's anger rises, and if he says to you, 'Why did you go so near the city to fight? Did you not know that they would shoot from the wall? Who killed Abimelech son of Jerubbaal? Did not a woman throw an upper millstone on him from the wall, so that he died at Thebez? Why did you go so near the wall?' then you shall say, 'Your servant Uriah the Hittite is dead too.'" . . . When the mourning was over, David sent and brought her to his house, and she became his wife, and bore him a son.

But the thing that David had done displeased the LORD and the LORD sent Nathan to David. . . . Nathan said to David, "You are the man! Thus says the LORD, the God of Israel: I anointed you king over Israel, and I rescued you from the hand of Saul; I gave you your master's house, and your master's wives into your bosom, and gave you the house of Israel and of Judah; and if that had been too little, I would have added as much more. Why have you despised the word of the LORD, to do what is evil in his sight? You have struck down Uriah the Hittite with the sword, and have taken his wife to be your wife, and have killed him with the sword of the Ammonites. Now therefore the sword shall never depart from your house, for you have despised me, and have taken the wife of Uriah the Hittite to be your wife. . . .

David said to Nathan, "I have sinned against the LORD." Nathan said to David, "Now the LORD has put away your sin; you shall not die. Nevertheless, because by this deed you have utterly scorned the LORD, the child that is born to you shall die." Then Nathan went to his house.

The LORD struck the child that Uriah's wife bore to David, and it became very ill. David therefore pleaded with God for the child; David fasted, and went in and lay all night on the ground. The elders of his house stood beside him, urging him to rise from the ground; but he would not, nor did he eat food with them. On the seventh day the child died. And the servants of David were afraid to tell him that the child was dead; for they said, "While the child was still alive, we spoke to him, and he did not listen to us; how then can we tell him the child is dead? He may do himself some harm." But when David saw that his servants were whispering together, he perceived that the child was dead; and David said to his servants, "Is the child dead?" They said, "He is dead."

Then David rose from the ground, washed, anointed himself, and changed his clothes. He went into the house of the LORD, and worshiped; he then went to his own house; and when he asked, they set food before him and he ate. Then his servants said to him, "What is this thing that you have done? You fasted and wept for the child while it was alive; but when the child died, you rose and ate food." He said, "While the child was still alive, I fasted and wept; for I said, 'Who knows? The LORD may be gracious to me, and the child may live.' But now he is dead; why should I fast? Can I bring him back again? I shall go to him, but he will not return to me."

Then David consoled his wife Bathsheba, and went to her, and lay with her; and she bore a son, and he named him Solomon. The LORD loved him, and sent a message by the prophet Nathan; so he named him Jedidiah, because of the LORD.

Commentary

"YOU ARE THE ONE."

The key images in this passage are the hard eyes, the jarring voice, and the pointing finger of Nathan as he confronts David in his sinfulness: "You are the one." Nathan was addressing David, king of Israel and Judah. That was David—artistic, full of charm, a poet, a musician, a military hero. David was everything anyone could ever aspire to be. God's hand had shaped the events of his life and had led him from victory to victory.

As the king of northern Israel and southern Judah, David wore a double crown. By the sheer force of his dynamic personality David welded into one nation the two disparate entities, and he established Jerusalem as the site of his capital. He was, in effect, the darling of Jerusalem. In addition, God had bestowed on David yet another, more enduring blessing: God promised him that the future of Israel's deepest hope would be secured in his descendants (2 Samuel 7:13).

For his part, David had been exemplary. In the first half of his life, he had been faithful to the unfolding of God's plan in the events that were shaping his destiny. Yet he sinned. At the pinnacle of his success, when life held the most promise, David was unfaithful. Even the king, even David, was not immune to sin!

Whereas the first book of Chronicles gives us an idealized picture of David, the author of the second book of Samuel shows us the paradox in David—the shadows as well as the light. Nathan's confrontation of David represents the moment in which David was forced to face that shadow, his sin.

Nathan's words pierced through David's egotistical facade and self-seeking. He challenged not only the grievous sexual sin of passion with Bathsheba, but also the deeper disposition of sin that unleashed that act and those that followed. David had proceeded with cold deliberation to control and manipulate people and circumstances for his own selfish purposes. Faced with his sin, David wept. He was unmasked. His carefully constructed defense system had collapsed.

He who was the defender of the poor and arbiter of justice had himself stolen from the poor and made a mockery of the law of justice and charity. He who was king experienced his own inner poverty and weakness. David was confronted with the painful reality that he had contributed to the power of evil. The moment of awareness became for David the moment of confession and conversion. David cried out, "I have sinned against Yahweh!"

David's experience of inner poverty became the stance of dependency before God. In the knowledge and acceptance of himself as sinner, David entered into a deeper reality. In the moment of submitting himself to God, he rose from his weeping and resumed his task as king and guardian of Israel. He was never more human, more royal, more truly a servant of God, than at the moment of surrender.

The challenge of the prophet had become for David the call to life.

Suggested Approach to Prayer

Daily Prayer Pattern

I quiet myself and relax in the presence of God.
I declare my dependence on God.

Grace

I ask for intense sorrow for my sinfulness.

Method: Contemplation

I contemplate in detail the scene between David and Nathan. I assume the role of David. I experience Nathan's finger pointing at me. I listen to his stern voice as he accuses me. I am "the one." As I become aware of my own sinfulness, I allow myself to feel, throughout my being, the weight of evil.

Closing

I see Christ on the cross. I speak to him from the depths of my awareness.

I close my prayer with the *Our Father.*

Review of Prayer

I write in my journal my feelings as I stand accused.

Week Two, Day 5
Out of the Depths

PSALM 130

Out of the depths I cry to you, O LORD.
  Lord, hear my voice!
Let your ears be attentive
  to the voice of my supplications!

If you, O LORD, should mark iniquities,
  Lord, who could stand?
But there is forgiveness with you,
  so that you may be revered.

I wait for the LORD, my soul waits,
  and in his word I hope;
my soul waits for the Lord
  more than those who watch for the morning,
  more than those who watch for the morning.

O Israel, hope in the LORD!
  For with the LORD there is steadfast love,
  and with him is great power to redeem.
It is he who will redeem Israel
  from all its iniquities.

Commentary

"OUT OF THE DEPTHS . . . *DE PROFUNDIS* . . . have I called to you, O LORD."

Psalm 130 represents a profound cry for mercy and relief on the part of an individual who is experiencing desperation. He is feeling totally isolated and cut off from all love and meaning. He is literally begging God to listen.

Has there not been for each of us a moment, a night, when that same cry was wrung from us? A cry like this could arise from a number of situations, any of which would plunge us into an acute experience of pain or loss.

The experience from which the psalmist cries out is the anguish of being alienated from God and others through personal sinfulness. He describes his anguish as coming from the depths. The "depths" may refer to the poignancy of loss that is experienced by those who are in Sheol, cast into the far-reaching, shadowy, after-death existence. The depths may also hold the many-faceted symbol of chaotic waters. For the Hebrew people, the sea represented not only death but also birth and new creation (Genesis 1:2).

Though his suffering is extreme, the psalmist is not without hope. We hear him acknowledge God's forgiveness in spite of his many sins. He is counting on that forgiveness and admitting that no one really could deserve it. He is aware that the record of everyone is so contaminated that only God's pure gift of mercy could lift them from the depths of misery.

"But there is forgiveness with you, so that you may be revered."

The hope is breathtaking. Not only does the psalmist count on God's forgiveness; he also knows that with the forgiveness comes a second favor. Where there is forgiveness, there follows a change of heart, there follows reverence.

Our English word *reverence* has lost some of the fullness of the Hebrew word in its root meaning. The original intention of *reverence*, as used in this passage, implies a fullness of religious experience such as would occur in *metanoia*, a total change of heart.

This reverence includes a dimension of fear. It is not anxious, flight-type fear as in the face of an impending danger. This is fear as awe or sense of wonder, which is inspired by one to whom we are strongly attracted, yet who is so far above us that our only authentic response is one of adoration.

The fear inspired by forgiveness is the harbinger, the messenger, that a new revelation of God has taken place. This revelation enables the repentant sinner to see God as he has never seen him before and to relate to him in a new way.

We can see an example of this "new way" of seeing and relating to God in the experience of Moses and the Israelite people during their time in the desert. After having received the tablets inscribed with the law, Moses returned to the people to find them engaged in the worship of false gods. Both God and Moses were outraged at the sin. Moses pleaded for his people.

In the moment of forgiveness, God gave a further revelation of himself: Moses "proclaimed the name, 'The LORD.' The LORD passed before him, and proclaimed, 'The LORD, the LORD, a God merciful and gracious, slow to anger, and abounding in steadfast love and faithfulness, keeping steadfast love for the thousandth generation, forgiving iniquity and transgression and sin, yet by no means clearing the guilty, but visiting the iniquity of the parents upon the children and the children's children, to the third and the fourth generation'" (Exodus 34:5–7).

To be forgiven is to see God and to be impelled to awe and loving gratitude to trust. And that is to worship. In the psalm, the sinner is awaiting the fullness of forgiveness he knows will come. He turns to the community of Israel and instructs them, also, to wait. Both he and Israel are experiencing the darkness of night, the absence of God. We need only remember our own experience of waiting in the night, how we kept looking for the darkness to give way to the first hint of morning light. Even more, the psalmist awaits the dawn of God's forgiveness. Through that forgiveness, he and the community will be restored and made whole in a new and renewed vision.

Suggested Approach to Prayer

Daily Prayer Pattern
I quiet myself and relax in the presence of God.
I declare my dependence on God.

Grace
I ask for a growing and intense sorrow for sin, even for the gift of tears.

Method
I pray this psalm out of the depths of my own sinfulness as I consider the following:

How my sin has alienated me from my self, has deprived me of my sense of worth, and has been an obstacle to my becoming the unique person God intends me to be

How the saints through their deliberate choices have become whole and holy, whereas I through my deliberate sinful choices have often fragmented and spiritually hurt myself

How, although I was created to be in close relationship with God, my Creator, and to be in harmony with and give praise with all creation, I have made choices to depend on myself alone and have, as a consequence, alienated myself from God, from others, and from creation

How my physical and intellectual limitations and fragility are often an experience of the effects of sin

How I have, through my sinfulness, contributed to the movement of evil in the world

Closing

I go before crucified Jesus and speak to him of whatever comes to mind and heart.

Review of Prayer

I write in my journal my growing sense of sorrow for my sinfulness.

Week Two, Day 6
God Is God

....

Job 42:1–6

Then Job answered the LORD:

"I know that you can do all things,

and that no purpose of yours can be thwarted.

'Who is this that hides counsel without knowledge?'

Therefore I have uttered what I did not understand,

　　things too wonderful for me, which I did not know.

'Hear, and I will speak;

　　I will question you, and you declare to me.'

I had heard of you by the hearing of the ear,

　　but now my eye sees you;

therefore I despise myself,

　　and repent in dust and ashes."

Commentary

JOB IS JOB, AND GOD is God. It is in this awareness that Job, at last, surrenders and finds joy. This simple assertion expresses the core message not only of verses 1–6 of chapter 42 but also of the entire book of Job.

These verses are the climax and resolution of Job's long and tortuous faith struggle. Job was a deeply religious man, influential and successful. He had a loving wife and family, owned vast properties, and had acquired wealth.

Satan challenged God by discrediting Job's faith. Satan made a wager with God that if Job were deprived of the comfort of his family, wealth, and influence, his faith would crumble. God agreed to the testing of Job's faith. Gradually, Job was stripped of his family, his possessions, and even his health.

Bewildered by his misfortunes, Job wrestled interiorly, seeking initially to understand what God's reasons might be for allowing him to be afflicted with such pain and suffering. The questions of "Why me?" and "What have I done to deserve this?" gave way to the deeper questions that were in reality an attempt to grasp and comprehend the inner heart and mind of God: Where is the justice of God? Why do the innocent suffer while the wicked prosper? Job's personal struggle raised him to a new level of consciousness: the enigma or paradox he experienced was part of a larger, cosmic question.

In the midst of Job's confusion, God spoke. In effect, he said, "Who do you think you are?" God's response was not one of self-defense, nor did it offer an easy solution to the paradox. Through the unanswerable questions that God put to Job, he led him to discover his own human limitations. God's questions pointed to the unfathomable wisdom and greatness revealed in creation.

Overcome with wonder before the greatness of God, Job surrendered. His former knowledge by hearsay had been surpassed by his personal encounter with God. Astounded, Job easily let go of his previous inadequate assumptions about God. No longer reliant on his own strength and integrity, his fears dissipated. Inspired with a new confidence, Job accepted his human limitations.

Job acknowledged that before God's wisdom, his own wisdom was ignorance; before God's power, his power was weakness;

before God's justice, his justice was unfairness; and in the light of God's love, his own love was revealed in all its pettiness. Job accepted the world as it really was, and through that acceptance, he received God as God (46, p. 441).

God is God, and Job is Job.

Suggested Approach to Prayer

Daily Prayer Pattern

I quiet myself and relax in the presence of God.
I declare my dependence on God.

Grace

I ask for a growing and intense sorrow for sin, even for the gift of tears.

Method: Meditation

I prayerfully reread the passage. I allow the words of Job's surrender to resonate deeply.

As I meditate on this passage in the light of my own human limitations and sinfulness, I consider the great contrast between God and myself. For example:

> *God's wisdom* and the times I felt I had to have all the answers—for the times when I have struggled to compensate for my lack of wisdom by impressing others with my knowledge, my degrees, and my facts.
>
> *God's justice* and the times I have been self-righteous or have blindly oppressed others—for the times when

I have engaged in overconsumption while criticizing and judging the injustice of others.

God's power and the times I have misused and corrupted the authority and influence with which I have been entrusted—for the times I have tried to manipulate and control other people and situations; my hunger for prestige.

God's love and the times I have been envious, suspicious, or lacking in trust; for the times I have given gifts with "strings attached"; for my harsh and petty words and actions.

Closing

I go before Jesus crucified, confiding to him the feelings and desires that arise within me and whatever else I am prompted to tell him.

I close with the Our Father.

Review of Prayer

I write in my journal my awareness and the feelings I have experienced in the reflection of contrasts between God and myself.

Week Three, Day 1
Homelessness

....

Ezekiel 36:25–29

I will sprinkle clean water upon you, and you shall be clean from all your uncleannesses, and from all your idols I will cleanse you. A new heart I will give you, and a new spirit I will put within you; and I will remove from your body the heart of stone and give you a heart of flesh. I will put my spirit within you, and make you follow my statutes and be careful to observe my ordinances. Then you shall live in the land that I gave to your ancestors; and you shall be my people, and I will be your God. I will save you from all your uncleannesses, and I will summon the grain and make it abundant and lay no famine upon you.

The Lord Yahweh speaks:
I will cleanse you;
I will pour water upon you;
I will give you a new heart;
I will remove your heart of stone;
I will put my spirit within you.

Commentary

IT IS THROUGH AND IN the holiness of God that Ezekiel shows us the Lord's commitment to restore his people and thereby to reestablish himself among the nations as the compassionate One who cares and has the power to rescue.

God was speaking to the Israelite people, who were in exile. They were in a strange land, separated from all they knew and all that gave meaning to their lives. Not only had their land been overtaken by a foreign power, but their homes and businesses, which they had been forced to leave, were taken over by strangers whom the foreign ruler had imported to repopulate the land.

Although they were without their homeland and no longer a political power, the greatest sadness of the exiled people lay in the knowledge that their temple, the center of their religious beliefs, had been burned to the ground. They had believed that Yahweh's presence was identified with the land and was focused within the temple. Living among a pagan people, they were deprived of all the familiar and cultural supports that had nurtured them and from which they had gained their own identity and meaning.

They viewed the traumatic experience of exile as the consequence and punishment for their unfaithfulness to God and their unfaithfulness to the covenant promise they had entered into with him. However, what appeared to be the end of everything became, instead, a new beginning. Under the leadership of the priest Ezekiel, who had accompanied them into exile, their experience of displacement became a vehicle for a new vision (Ezekiel 1:4–28).

Ezekiel had carried into exile the sacred scrolls on which were recorded their stories and history. Under his direction they recalled those stories, looked within their hearts, and found there the following questions: What are we doing here? Where is our God now? To what are we being called?

In the midst of their searching, plunged into the abyss of the pain of their own nothingness, they were wrenched free by a new vision of God. God spoke, and they heard. They heard *their* God, the God of Abraham, Isaac, and Jacob, speaking a new promise: "I will give you a new heart and a new spirit."

The God who spoke to the Israelite people in exile is the same God who speaks to us. And his message remains constant: He is *our* God, and we are his people. God speaks to us in our exile. We, as a people, have our own experience of homelessness.

This was poignantly captured in the tender figure of the extraterrestrial E.T., in the pathos of his longing to return home. Millions who viewed this film identified with E.T.'s longing for home. "Home," in this sense, carries the fuller dimension of being in harmony with our deepest selves, with one another, with the earth, and with God.

All that we are, historically and physically, moves us toward harmony. Where our personal choices and decisions work against that movement, we experience a radical homelessness or exile—an alienation that is the core of sin. In spite of our human frailty and our personal and communal history of sin, God always stands ready to act in and through the human heart.

The human heart, rather than the head, was for the Hebrews the center of thought and decision. God acts in the human heart—in its knowing, valuing, and choosing—to move forward the harmony and fruitfulness of our world. In the submission to God's active will, the human heart becomes the new temple of the holiness of God. For us, as for the exiled people, the "new creation is dependent on our willingness to choose life—to say yes to taking on the task the God of history puts before us" (53, p. 394).

Suggested Approach to Prayer

Daily Prayer Pattern
I quiet myself and relax in the presence of God.
I declare my dependence on God.

Grace
I ask God for the gift of growing and intense sorrow for my sins, even of tears.

Method
Prayerfully I reread the passage from Ezekiel, allowing God's reassuring words to wash over me.

I consider how, in spite of my sinfulness, God has supported and given me life to this very moment. I consider how he continues to renew my heart

> through the beauty and life-giving nature of the earth—the air, water, soil
>
> through the enjoyment and service of the great variety of plants and animals
>
> through the goodness, love, and prayer of family and friends

Finally, I consider with amazement this paradox: I am a sinner, unfaithful in so many ways, yet at the same time I am the recipient of so much goodness and love.

Closing

I place myself before Jesus crucified and let my heart speak. I give thanks for his great mercy to me.

I close my prayer with the Our Father.

Review of Prayer

I write in my journal any feelings, experiences, or insights that have come to my awareness during this prayer period.

Week Three, Day 2
A Cry for Mercy

....

Psalm 51

Have mercy on me, O God,
  according to your steadfast love;
according to your abundant mercy
  blot out my transgressions.
Wash me thoroughly from my iniquity,
  and cleanse me from my sin.

For I know my transgressions,
  and my sin is ever before me.
Against you, you alone, have I sinned,
  and done what is evil in your sight,
so that you are justified in your sentence
  and blameless when you pass judgment.
Indeed, I was born guilty,
  a sinner when my mother conceived me.

You desire truth in the inward being;
  therefore teach me wisdom in my secret heart.
Purge me with hyssop, and I shall be clean;
  wash me, and I shall be whiter than snow.
Let me hear joy and gladness;
  let the bones that you have crushed rejoice.

Hide your face from my sins,
    and blot out all my iniquities.

Create in me a clean heart, O God,
    and put a new and right spirit within me.
Do not cast me away from your presence,
    and do not take your holy spirit from me.
Restore to me the joy of your salvation,
    and sustain in me a willing spirit.

Then I will teach transgressors your ways,
    and sinners will return to you.
Deliver me from bloodshed, O God,
    O God of my salvation,
    and my tongue will sing aloud of your deliverance.

O Lord, open my lips,
    and my mouth will declare your praise.
For you have no delight in sacrifice;
    if I were to give a burnt offering, you would not be pleased.
The sacrifice acceptable to God is a broken spirit;
    a broken and contrite heart, O God, you will not despise.

Do good to Zion in your good pleasure;
    rebuild the walls of Jerusalem,
then you will delight in right sacrifices,
    in burnt offerings and whole burnt offerings;
    then bulls will be offered on your altar.

Commentary

THIS PSALM IS TRULY A prayer of the heart, rising from the innermost being of someone who has personally experienced the harsh realities of sin in his or her life. It expresses a keen awareness of the ramifications of personal sin and reveals a deep need and longing for spiritual cleansing and forgiveness.

Commonly know as the *Miserere*, Psalm 51 is the fourth of the seven penitential psalms. It has been used for centuries in the penitential liturgies of the church. Traditionally, it has been identified as the prayer and lament of David as he pleaded forgiveness for his sin with Bathsheba. In its present form, however, it comes from a later time, beautifully rendering the wisdom and hopes of Jeremiah and Ezekiel, prophets of the Exile. Timeless in its images of yearning, it has been a source of consolation and guidance for countless people in their personal passage from the despair of sin to the joy of forgiveness, and from fragmentation to wholeness. For men and women of the twenty-first century, the psalm can be seen as the desire and need to integrate the physical, psychological, and spiritual dimensions of our humanity.

The psalm begins with an image-laden plea for mercy and forgiveness. In its English translation, the psalm loses some of its impact. The Hebrew text reveals three specific types of sins being confessed: conscious rebellion, translated as "faults"; the sin of error, translated as "guilt"; and sin as a "going astray," translated simply as "sin."

Paralleling the three areas of sinfulness, we hear the psalmist make three pleas for forgiveness in a triple image of cleansing.

He prays that his sins of rebellion may be "wiped away," that his sins of error be "washed away," and that his sins of going astray may be "purified."

Once again the imagery is dulled in the English translation. The "wiping away" as well as the "purifying" refer to the temple rituals and ceremonial declarations of forgiveness or innocence. The particular Hebraic word used for "washing" has the connotation of vigorous scrubbing, such as the Israelite women did when washing their clothes by beating them with stones in cold water (68, p. 258). The psalmist clearly relates a sincere desire for interior cleansing!

Verses 3 and 4 echo the beautiful passage of Exodus 34:6–7 in which God is described not only as loving but also as allowing nothing to go unchecked. God does listen to the plea for mercy. He is faithful; he allows the effects of sin, the alchemy of suffering, to take its transforming course.

Verse 5, which states that the sinner was guilty from the moment of conception, is not a commentary on the morality of sexuality, nor does it allude to the doctrine of original sin. Rather, the intended meaning is to convey the tendency of all of us as humans toward rebellion, error, and inadequacy.

"You desire truth in the inward being; therefore teach me wisdom in my secret heart." The connection of verse 6 with verse 5 is made clear if we hear an alternate translation: "Indeed you are pleased with fidelity amid [conjugal] intimacy; in such secret acts you impart the experience of [wondrous] wisdom" (68, p. 259). Just as new life is conceived in the intimacy of conjugal union, so too new birth—spiritual renewal—is conceived when the heart of the sinner becomes receptive to God's life-giving power.

The remainder of the psalm continues in its plea for forgiveness and renewal. It is permeated with trust and the anticipation of joy. The psalmist desires to be so appalled at this sinfulness that he will forever be purged of entertaining even the mere idea of sinning again!

He turns to the Lord, asking that he be given the grace of healing that was symbolized in the sprinkling with hyssop. Hyssop is a fragrant, medicinal herb that was commonly used in ritual cleansing. With that healing the psalmist is hopeful that his interior anguish, which he undoubtedly is experiencing even in his body as a crushing weight, will be lifted.

"The sacrifice acceptable to God is a broken spirit." Only in the recesses of a heart broken open with sorrow and filled with determination can authentic healing and joy be born. Without this interior ripening and mature commitment, all the ritual of organized religion is empty.

"Create in me a clean heart, O God." Psalm 51, in its totality, is a cry for wholeness and an announcement of a new beginning. The word *create, bará,* is the same word used in the first creation account found in Genesis. The energy that was the pulsating force of cosmic creation is the same regenerative force present in the repentant and healed heart. Rooted in the compassion of God, we are given new life and become whole. In both word and deed, we express our praise to God.

Suggested Approach to Prayer

Daily Prayer Pattern
I quiet myself and relax in the presence of God.
I declare my dependence on God.

Grace

I ask for the grace of intense sorrow for all my sins.

Method: Meditation

I prayerfully read the psalms, aloud if possible, as if the words were my own. I allow the yearning within my heart to find expression through the words of the psalmist. I linger with the verses that speak to me most profoundly.

Closing

I go before Christ crucified and tell him of my yearnings for healing and peace.

I close my prayer with the Our Father.

Review of Prayer

I write in my journal the words of the psalm that have most deeply expressed my own longings.

Week Three, Day 3

Repetition

....

Suggested Approach to Prayer

Daily Prayer Pattern

I quiet myself and relax in the presence of God.
I declare my dependence on God.

Grace

I ask for a growing and intense sorrow for my sins, even for the gift of tears.

Method: Repetition

In preparation, I review my previous prayer periods by reading my journal since the last repetition day. I select for my repetition the period of prayer in which I was most deeply moved or the one in which I experienced dryness—that is, a lack of emotional response. I use the method with which I approached the passage initially. I open myself to hear again God's word to me in that particular passage.

Review of Prayer

I write in my journal any feelings, experiences, or insights that have surfaced in this second "listening."

Part Three

The Roots of
Personal Sinfulness

Week Three, Day 4

The Decision to Love

....

MATTHEW 25:31–46

"When the Son of Man comes in his glory, and all the angels with him, then he will sit on the throne of his glory. All the nations will be gathered before him, and he will separate people one from another as a shepherd separates the sheep from the goats, and he will put the sheep at his right hand and the goats at the left. Then the king will say to those at his right hand, 'Come, you that are blessed by my Father, inherit the kingdom prepared for you from the foundation of the world; for I was hungry and you gave me food, I was thirsty and you gave me something to drink, I was a stranger and you welcomed me, I was naked and you gave me clothing, I was sick and you took care of me, I was in prison and you visited me.' Then the righteous will answer him, 'Lord, when was it that we saw you hungry and gave you food, or thirsty and gave you something to drink? And when was it that we saw you a stranger and welcomed you, or naked and gave you clothing? And when was it that we saw you sick or in prison and visited you?' And the king will answer them, 'Truly I tell you, just as you did it to one of the least of these who are members of my family, you did it to me.' Then he will say to those at his left hand, 'You that are accursed, depart from me into the eternal fire prepared for the devil and his angels; for I was hungry and you gave me no food, I was thirsty and you gave me nothing to drink, I was a stranger and you did not welcome me, naked and you did not give me clothing, sick and in prison and you did not visit me.' Then they also will answer,

'Lord, when was it that we saw you hungry or thirsty or a stranger or naked or sick or in prison, and did not take care of you?' Then he will answer them, 'Truly I tell you, just as you did not do it to one of the least of these, you did not do it to me.' And these will go away into eternal punishment, but the righteous into eternal life.'"

Commentary

THIS PASSAGE BRINGS TO MIND a woman in northwestern Minnesota who is known and loved by many. She grew up in poverty. Housing was inadequate, and food was sometimes scarce. Even as a child, she decided that when she grew up, she would find a way to care for the poor. That decision has influenced and given direction to her entire adult life. Daily she is involved with serving the needs of the poor. She and others who have joined her provide food, clothing, and shelter—as well as hope—to the many who come to her in their need.

The decision to actively love those in need is at the heart of this passage. On that decision rests our ultimate judgment. Our saying yes to love is saying yes to our own fullness in Christ.

This passage is one of the final instructions of Jesus to his disciples shortly before he entered into his passion. He told them that to enter into union with him, they must be engaged in actively meeting the needs of others, particularly the poor and oppressed. This is the theme also found in Jesus' farewell message to his disciples in the Gospel of John (see John 13).

Although delivered to the inner circle of disciples, this directive is of universal import. It is meant for all nations and all people, and it is timeless in its scope and relevance. Each of us is faced daily with the needs of those around us. The woman mentioned earlier might appear to have an extraordinary commitment to loving the poor, and she does. However, if we were to view life from the perspective of this passage, we would begin to see that our lives, too, are extraordinary.

The commitment of marriage, parenthood, and profession is *extra*ordinary! Within each life commitment, we face the daily needs of the people to whom we are committed. Their "poverty"—their brokenness and limitations—are a call to love. The poverty of those around us in ordinary circumstances may be less dramatic but, by that fact, more demanding. Jesus calls us to love in the simple things; it is an uncalculating love, free of self-interest, the spontaneous response of a loving heart.

In this passage from Matthew's Gospel, Jesus says that when we respond in love, we are responding to him. We are responding not *as though* he were present but to his *actual* presence. Jesus has so identified himself with the poor and suffering that, in the deepest sense, he is present within their suffering and is the recipient of the love that is extended.

This revelation is as astonishing to us as it was to his first disciples. It is a mysterious, wondrous occurrence that in loving one another, we recognize and serve Christ. The paradox is that although the Christ in this passage is exalted and glorified—"the Son of Man"—he is the one who identifies with the poor.

If we could hear this message, if we truly could accept and assimilate it, it would turn the world upside down! It challenges our contemporary value system, which emphasizes achievement and success. We are often preoccupied with perfection. This preoccupation deprives us of wholeness and leads us into the self-made hell that is separation from ourselves, from one another, and from God.

If the presence of Christ in one another is astonishing, no less is the fact that each of us has been given the freedom to make choices that lead to the discovery of our wholeness and Christ's presence within us. Too often, however, we use as an excuse our "fate"—the circumstances of our life—to settle into rigid and inflexible ways of living and acting. We cling to this excuse because we deny that we have the courage to change.

Jesus did not accept the excuses of those who were separated and "on his left," and he will not accept our excuses. He will, however, accept us with our brokenness and limitations. We need to claim the courage to abandon ourselves with trust to his love and creative grace.

As followers of Jesus and believers in his resurrection, we dare not allow our freedom to be restricted or predetermined by whatever suffering and limitation we encounter. Past inadequate decisions and sinful responses, our own and those of others, cannot be excuses and need not be obstacles to fullness of life.

It is a false assumption that the past predetermines us. If we believe that, then we choose debilitation, destruction, and death. Within our poverty, we stand free. To reject that freedom is to reject Christ, and that is sin! This passage places upon each Christian the personal responsibility to love, by following Christ of the poor. Only in choosing to love do we recognize Jesus and realize life.

Suggested Approach to Prayer

Daily Prayer Pattern
I quiet myself and relax in the presence of God.
I declare my dependence on God.

Grace

I ask for a deepening awareness of the roots of my sinfulness, and for a growing sorrow.

Method

I take my place among the followers of Jesus. I listen intently to his words. I observe his facial expressions as he speaks to us. As I listen, I become aware of a day in my life and the people I meet there—spouse, family, friends, coworkers. I am aware of my patterns of interacting with each one. Then I hear Jesus describe the consequences of not loving. I ask myself, "How have I responded? Am I sent to his right hand as one who is deeply aware of and responsive to the real needs of others? Or am I with those dismissed to his left hand? In what ways have I been unaware, and therefore lacking in true love and responsiveness to others? How am I being called to love? What are the distractions that have preoccupied my attention and served as obstacles to my loving others?"

Closing

I close my prayer with a threefold conversation.

I turn to Mary who, with us, forms part of the community of all who have followed or now follow Christ. As mother of Jesus, she holds a special place in the communion of saints. In my own words, I ask her to obtain for me the gifts of

> a deep knowledge of my sinfulness and a hatred of sin
>
> an insight into the disorder in my life so that I may know how to refashion my life in the spirit of Jesus

an awareness of whatever may distract and separate me from Christ, so that I may let go of all that deflects me from him

I turn to Jesus, begging him to ask the Father in his name for these same gifts for me.

I turn to God the Father, that he who loved us so much that he sent his only Son will give me these same graces.

I pray the Our Father.

Review of Prayer

I write in my journal the feelings, experiences, and insights that surfaced within me during this period of prayer.

Week Three, Day 5

The Struggle

....

Romans 7:14–25

For we know that the law is spiritual; but I am of the flesh, sold into slavery under sin. I do not understand my own actions. For I do not do what I want, but I do the very thing I hate. Now if I do what I do not want, I agree that the law is good. But in fact it is no longer I that do it, but sin that dwells within me. For I know that nothing good dwells within me, that is, in my flesh. I can will what is right, but I cannot do it. For I do not do the good I want, but the evil I do not want is what I do. Now if I do what I do not want, it is no longer I that do it, but sin that dwells within me.

So I find it to be a law that when I want to do what is good, evil lies close at hand. For I delight in the law of God in my inmost self, but I see in my members another law at war with the law of my mind, making me captive to the law of sin that dwells in my members. Wretched man that I am! Who will rescue me from this body of death? Thanks be to God through Jesus Christ our Lord!

So then, with my mind I am a slave to the law of God, but with my flesh I am a slave to the law of sin.

Commentary

"Now why did I do that?"

"It just slipped out!"

"I didn't mean to do that!"

Each of us can identify with the Jekyll-and-Hyde frustration of St. Paul, not doing what he intended and not intending what he did. For us, as for Paul, the predicament is not amusing. Like Paul, we feel a restless spirit within us that acts, at times, contrary to our truer self. It is our shadow self.

Since earliest times, men and woman have wrestled with the conflict between good and evil. It is the mystery that religion has sought to unravel, the question philosophers have pondered, and the theme of the world's greatest works of art. In the myths, the dramas, the epics, and the novels of every era, we vicariously identify with those ensnared in this web.

Perhaps no other poet has so masterfully depicted the psychological subtleties and potential tragedies of this conflict as Shakespeare. In *Othello*, Shakespeare shows us a man caught between the innocent trust of the beautiful Desdemona and the cunning evil of Iago, his plotting subordinate. Othello allows himself to be tempted by the manipulative innuendos of Iago, who casts seeds of doubt as to Desdemona's faithfulness.

Othello succumbs. In the belief that her death will rid the earth of an evil influence, Othello strangles Desdemona. Only when it is too late does he realize that he has killed the one person who has loved him without reservation. He recognizes and claims the evil within himself. In anguish he cries out, "Roast me in sulfur! Wash me in steep-down gulfs of liquid fire! O Desdemona! Desdemona! dead! Oh! Oh! Oh!" (act 5, scene 2).

In movies such as the famous trilogies *Star Wars* and *The Lord of the Rings*, we see the forces of good and evil battle for control. The stark contrasting realities between good and evil are often depicted visually: good as translucent light and empowering strength, evil as foreboding darkness and satanic control.

This drama is played out in each of our lives. We do have, within us, a shadow self. Contemporary psychology has emphatically recognized and encouraged us to encounter it. If we repress or deny this negative side of ourselves, we become increasingly vulnerable to its influence, as was Othello. With Paul, we ask, "Who will rescue me?"

It is always a temptation to look to the law as an absolute assurance of safety, righteousness, and security. Law, which in theory is meant only to support what reason and wisdom show us to be right, when viewed as an entity unto itself actually cripples and fixates us. The law cannot save us! What is saving is not some*thing* but some*one*.

The consoling and extraordinary reality is that the someone is Jesus, crucified and risen. The mystery is that his risen Spirit lives in us as the source of our freedom and hope. "In him we live and move and have our being" (Acts 17:28).

Suggested Approach to Prayer

Daily Prayer Pattern
I quiet myself and relax in the presence of God.
I declare my dependence on God.

Grace
I ask for a deepening awareness of the roots of my sinfulness and for a growing sorrow.

Method

I enter into the confession of St. Paul, as I slowly, prayerfully read Romans 7:14–25, allowing the words to penetrate deeply into my awareness, opening my heart to the feelings and images his words evoke as I make them my own.

Closing

I close my prayer with a threefold conversation

I turn to Mary who, with us, forms part of the community of all who have followed or do follow Christ. As mother of Jesus, she holds a special place in the communion of saints. In my own words, I ask her to obtain for me the gifts of

> a deep knowledge of my sinfulness and a hatred for sin
>
> an insight into the disorder in my life so that I may know how to refashion my life in the spirit of Jesus
>
> an awareness of whatever may distract and separate me from Christ, so that I may let go of all that deflects me from him

I turn to Jesus, begging him to ask the Father in his name for these same gifts for me.

I turn to God the Father, that he who loved us so much that he sent his only Son will give me these same graces.

I pray the *Our Father.*

Review of Prayer

I record in my journal the feelings, experiences, and insights that surfaced during this period of prayer.

Week Three, Day 6

You Must Choose!

....

1 John 2:12–17

I am writing to you, little children,

    because your sins are forgiven on account of his name.

I am writing to you, fathers,

    because you know him who is from the beginning.

I am writing to you, young people,

    because you have conquered the evil one.

I write to you, children,

    because you know the Father.

I write to you, fathers,

    because you know him who is from the beginning.

I write to you, young people,

    because you are strong

    and the word of God abides in you,

    and you have overcome the evil one.

Do not love the world or the things in the world. The love of the Father is not in those who love the world; for all that is in the world—the desire of the flesh, the desire of the eyes, the pride in riches—comes not from the Father but from the world. And the world and its desire are passing away, but those who do the will of God live forever.

Commentary

"CONGRATULATIONS, SON. I'M PROUD OF you. You've made the right choice. It's worth everything you've had to do without; every effort you have made will be rewarded."

If you were at a reception following commencement exercises and mingled with the parents and graduates, you would repeatedly overhear these words of praise. You would be touched with the poignancy of the moment. It is as if all the love and hope that the parents had held, dreamed of, worked and sacrificed for, had been realized. In his affectionate words of congratulations, we sense the transparent bond between father and son. Our casual eavesdropping has made us privy to a father's unique moment of joy.

The warmth of the father's affirming words to his son is not unlike the spirit and message we hear St. John address to an early Christian community. As John speaks to all those he has nurtured in the faith, he calls them his own dear children.

Within the assembly, he then focuses on two specific groups who make up the community. One group is the elders who, not because of their age but on account of the longer duration of their membership, are called fathers. The newly baptized that make up the second group are called young men.

Like the father of the graduate, John affirms those he loves. He rejoices in the good work that has been begun in them. He recalls firmly that by placing their trust in Jesus, they have made the best possible choice.

Now he holds before them all the blessings they and the community have received as a consequence of their faith in the name—that is, in the power—of Jesus Christ. In the presence of Jesus, in an intimate relationship with him, they experience the peace that flows from knowing themselves as forgiven.

In declaring their dependence on God, they are empowered with the strength and ability not only to overcome evil in themselves but also to effect goodness in others. Through this union with Christ they grow in an interior knowledge of God, whose word has made its home in them.

If we were to continue to listen to the father as he spoke to his son at the reception, the words of praise would probably be followed by words of warning: "Be careful, and remember all you've learned. It won't be easy out there in the real world." This is precisely what John is saying to the community. He is warning them about the *world*: "You must not love this passing world."

John's use of the word *world* needs to be explored. John is *not* implying that Christians do not or should not love the world in which they live. God created the entire universe, the earth, and all it contains out of his immense love. The world is good. Jesus himself cherished a loving regard for nature, often drawing on the images of the world for his parables and teachings.

While reading John, we need to keep in mind that his use of the word *world* carried a negative connotation. The Greek word was *kosmos*, and the word had gradually taken on the burden of a negative moral value. It implied the world as alienated and separated from God. The Second Vatican Council noted that in this context, the term *world* means "that spirit of vanity and malice which transforms into an instrument of sin those human energies intended for the service of God and man" (*Gaudium et Spes*, 37). For John, the choice is very clear. It is as if he is saying, "You can't have it both ways. It is either God or the 'world.' You must choose!"

Apart from God, the world is contaminated. As a part of the world, we, too, have been exposed to and share in that process of degeneration. While our basic instincts are good and essential to our well-being, at the same time they are vulnerable in specific areas. There is within each of us a tendency to excess and exaggeration, particularly in regard to our pursuit of pleasure, our grasping for power, and in our accumulation of possessions. John speaks of these three areas of vulnerability as *"the desire of the flesh, the desire of the eyes, the pride in riches."* This is John's understanding of the world against which he warns his community.

It is impossible for us to isolate ourselves from our own humanness and from the world in which we live. Our only shield of protection can come from the surrender and total acceptance of God's love and grace as it comes to us through Christ.

Suggested Approach to Prayer

Daily Prayer Pattern
I quiet myself and relax in the presence of God.
I declare my dependence on God.

Grace
I ask God for a deepening awareness of the roots of my sinfulness and for a growing sorrow.

Method
As I slowly reread the letter of John, I experience him addressing his words to me, inviting me to reflect on the ways in which I have been affected by the "world" in which I live.

I consider how I have participated and contributed to the disorder and corruption that characterize a world separated from God.

Keeping in mind the three areas of vulnerability that John refers to—pursuit of pleasure, the grasp for power, and the accumulation of possessions—I reflect on the following list to be able to identify in myself the behavioral patterns that reveal to me any underlying dispositions or even predispositions that I may have toward more serious sins.

I keep in perspective the erosion of character and attitude begins in the small things of daily life. According to one spiritual writer, here are some of the things we would do well to meditate on:

> impatience; coarseness; lack of cleanliness; cheap literature; talkativeness; laughing at the faults of others; petty egotism in everyday life; petty enmities; over-sensitiveness; wasting time; cowardice; lack of respect for holy things; harmful spite portraying itself as a clever joke; stubbornness and obstinacy; moodiness that others must put up with; disorder in work; postponement of the unpleasant; gossip, conceit and self-praise; unjust preference for certain people that we find quite pleasant; hastiness in judging; false self-satisfaction; laziness; the tendency to give up learning any more; the tendency to refuse to listen to others. (59, p. 61)

Other things to consider include compulsive and excessive buying; overeating or drinking too much; a constant need to be the best, the first, or right; a preoccupation with appearance; bad manners; reading sleazy magazines and watching trashy television; negative, excessive, or petty criticism; uncontrollable or manipulative anger; masked hostilities; and sexist language or attitudes.

Closing

I close my prayer with a threefold conversation.

I turn to Mary who, with us, forms part of the community of all who have followed or do follow Christ. As mother of Jesus, she holds a special place in the communion of saints. In my own words, I ask her to obtain for me the gifts of

> a deep knowledge of my sinfulness and a hatred for sin
>
> an insight into the disorder in my life so that I may know how to refashion my life in the spirit of Jesus
>
> an awareness of whatever may distract and separate me from Christ, so that I may let go of all that deflects me from him

I turn to Jesus, begging him to ask the Father in his name for these same gifts for me.

I turn to God the Father, that he who loved us so much that he sent his only Son will give me these same graces.

I pray the Our Father.

Review of Prayer

After reflecting prayerfully on John's words and on the list of sinful behavior patterns, I record in my journal the tendencies I have toward certain areas of sinfulness. I take particular note of those that had not occurred to me previously.

Week Four, Day 1

Seduction

....

JAMES 1:13–18

No one, when tempted, should say, "I am being tempted by God"; for God cannot be tempted by evil and he himself tempts no one. But one is tempted by one's own desire, being lured and enticed by it; then, when that desire has conceived, it gives birth to sin, and that sin, when it is fully grown, gives birth to death. Do not be deceived, my beloved.

Every generous act of giving, with every perfect gift, is from above, coming down from the Father of lights, with whom there is no variation or shadow due to change. In fulfillment of his own purpose he gave us birth by the word of truth, so that we would become a kind of first fruits of his creatures.

Commentary

JAMES SPEAKS OF HOW SIN makes its insidious entry into our lives and can ultimately destroy us. A poignant commentary on this passage has been offered to us by a woman who recalls her painful journey through addiction and into new life:

> To take the very first sip of wine? There was excitement, desire, and curiosity. The wine sparkled in the crystal goblet and those around were drinking comfortably.
>
> I, too, sipped the wine. It was warm. I drained the glass. What comfort. It was wonderful; I

no longer felt depressed! I was giddy with happiness.

After dinner, I drank more wine and found myself "high" and funny! What power I had to make the others laugh with my funny words— I, who as my usual depressed self, was never funny. I learned a twofold lesson that night: wine relieves depression and gives one power.

That first drink of wine was pure innocence; what would come of it, no one would have guessed. So powerful was the lesson that I wanted to repeat it. I did not want to deal with the depression or its cause. I was evading the roots of the problem that had begun as someone else's mistake, a sin foisted on a young child.

Yet that mistake and that sin had continued to haunt me in my young adulthood. It came as denial, depression, and unhappiness. How would I escape? Relief seemed to lie in the direction of suicide, or the wine gulped to achieve a "high."

The seduction of the wine was the need for an instant and easy relief from the pain of living with unresolved hate, hurt, and guilt. Nothing better came along. Soon, very soon, the ravages of alcoholism caught me in a tidal wave of destruction. God would not help me, I said, since *he* didn't care. God was a "he" and I had been crushed by a "he."

It was not wrong for me to desire peace within my heart instead of the civil wars that raged there. My methods to attain serenity were wrong—I turned from alcohol to tranquilizers to pain pills. Addicted to these outside forces and under their control, I was being propelled toward a premature death.

Gradually the drugs quit working for me. They had turned on me. I got more and more depressed. Not only could I not trust God, parents, or friends, even drugs betrayed me.

I came as close to death at my own hands as I ever care to. The child of alcoholism is death: spiritual, emotional, and physical death. I almost completed the latter and had already experienced the first two.

When I awoke in an ICU bed and was told I was "lucky" to be alive, something took hold inside of me. In the previous night with the waves of pain from the overdose and the thought that I was dying, I had said to myself, "Well, *you* did this—*you* did it—are you ready to die?" Finally, I took responsibility for my life and possible death.

As I recuperated over the next few weeks, I let God into my life. I said, "Who am I to say that God does not care for me? Let him decide." From those first faltering steps back to the Light, growth has occurred in direct proportion to my relationship with God. On the road to recovery, I became aware of God's faithfulness. God is always there— ready to help, to heal, always loving us.

Serenity, peace, and calmness are now more the rule, and the civil wars are over. I dealt with the source of the depression and the God of healing, who forgives all sin, graced me with forgiveness for those in my life who had injured me. I need not be devastated for life because of someone else's mistakes and sins. What freedom!

Suggested Approach to Prayer

Daily Prayer Pattern

I quiet myself and relax in the presence of God.
I declare my dependence on God.

Grace

I ask for a keen awareness of the roots of my sinfulness and for a growing sorrow.

Method

I prayerfully reread the words of James.

I become aware of an area of sinfulness in my life, recalling from the past the first instances of seduction and how it has grown like a virus and infected so many aspects of my life, such as ministry, self-esteem, prayer, or relationships.

Closing

I close my prayer with a threefold conversation.

I turn to Mary who, with us, forms part of the community of all who have followed or do follow Christ. As mother of Jesus, she holds a special place in the communion of saints. In my own words, I ask her to obtain for me the gifts of

> a deep knowledge of my sinfulness and a hatred of sin
>
> an insight into the disorder in my life so that I may know how to refashion my life in the spirit of Jesus
>
> an awareness of whatever may distract and separate me from Christ, so that I may let go of all that deflects me from him

I turn to Jesus, begging him to ask the Father in his name for these same gifts for me.

I turn to God the Father, that he who loved us so much that he sent his only Son will give me these same graces.

I pray the Our Father.

Review of Prayer

I record in my journal any new awareness of how seduction to sin has influenced me and how God is drawing me to himself.

Week Four, Day 2
Blessing or Curse?

....

JAMES 3:2–12

For all of us make many mistakes. Anyone who makes no mistakes in speaking is perfect, able to keep the whole body in check with a bridle. If we put bits into the mouths of horses to make them obey us, we guide their whole bodies. Or look at ships: though they are so large that it takes strong winds to drive them, yet they are guided by a very small rudder wherever the will of the pilot directs. So also the tongue is a small member, yet it boasts of great exploits.

How great a forest is set ablaze by a small fire! And the tongue is a fire. The tongue is placed among our members as a world of iniquity; it stains the whole body, sets on fire the cycle of nature, and is itself set on fire by hell. For every species of beast and bird, of reptile and sea creature, can be tamed and has been tamed by the human species, but no one can tame the tongue—a restless evil, full of deadly poison. With it we bless the Lord and Father, and with it we curse those who are made in the likeness of God. From the same mouth come blessing and cursing. My brothers and sisters, this ought not to be so. Does a spring pour forth from the same opening both fresh and brackish water? Can a fig tree, my brothers and sisters, yield olives, or a grapevine figs? No more can salt water yield fresh.

Commentary

THIS PASSAGE IN THE LETTER of James calls our attention to our speech. Unfortunately, the tongue can become an abusive and devastating weapon that issues forth its own particular spray of death and that incites within us an undeniable fear and alarm.

The tongue can kill. It has the capacity to cut down or totally deface a person. With caustic harshness, or sometimes more subtly like a smooth knife, it can destroy people's lives, sever relationships, and split apart entire communities. The potential death-dealing power of the tongue must not be underestimated.

"Many have fallen by the edge of the sword, but not as many as have fallen because of the tongue. . . . [I]ts death is an evil death" (Sirach 28:18, 21). This quotation from the book of Sirach confirms James's denunciation of speech misused. James makes it clear that all of us fall into undisciplined, loose habits of speaking. It happens over and over. In using the images of bit and rudder, he illustrates for us the necessity for decisive control. Repeatedly, we must become aware of the power of the human tongue and the potential there is for good or evil in the gift of speech.

Just as the rider controls the horse by the bit in the horse's mouth, and just as the pilot guides the course of the ship by use of the rudder, the will gives direction to the tongue. The will is the means by which we exercise our responsibility in speaking. In assuming that responsibility, in bringing our speech under the direction of our free and conscious choice, every aspect of our lives benefits from and results in an increased coordination and focus. As James says, "If we put bits into the mouths of horses to make them obey us, we guide their whole bodies"!

The exercise of the will is key in the process of becoming fully human. From birth to death, we are haunted by an innate lack of discipline, which causes us to do things we don't intend. We can offset these pernicious tendencies when we consciously exercise our will.

From the one source comes the potential for good or evil. The speaking of a word immediately releases energy that sets into motion the intended effect, whether good or evil, blessing or curse. James urges us to choose wisely. When we choose to bless, we save ourselves from the destructive fire that evil ignites—a fire that spreads throughout all creation.

Do not neglect the gift that is in you. . . . Put these things into practice, devote yourself to them, so that all may see your progress. Pay close attention to yourself and to your teaching [your speech]; continue in these things, for in doing this you will save both yourself and your hearers.

1 TIMOTHY 4:14–16

In faith, the individual act of will frees the gift of speech for its intended purpose: praise and blessings.

Suggested Approach to Prayer

Daily Prayer Pattern
I quiet myself and relax in the presence of God.
I declare my dependence on God.

Grace
I ask God for a deepening awareness of the roots of my sinfulness and for a growing sorrow.

Method
In light of the passage in James on the use and abuse of the tongue, and in light of the significance of the will, I prayerfully

consider the role and exercise of will in my life, particularly as it relates to speech. I ask God to make me aware of the areas in which I need to be strengthened.

I begin by taking a look at my will and asking whether it is frequently

> pushed around by the will of other people
>
> subjugated by my feelings, such as depression, anger, or fear
>
> paralyzed by inertia
>
> lulled to sleep by habit
>
> disintegrated by distractions
>
> corroded by doubts

Do I generally do what I wish, from the depths of my being, because I have willed it, or does some other factor prevail?

I take some time to consider the major aspects of my life and my most important relationships. I write down my answers in detail. *

I reflect on the patterns of speech on any particular day. Have my words been a blessing or a curse? As I become aware of the disorder of speech in my life and my need to strengthen my will in that regard, I consider, from among the following, an action or actions that would be most appropriate for me. I adopt and practice the actions on a daily basis until new—and blessed— habits of speech become more natural and spontaneous.

---

*Taken with permission from Piero Ferrucci, *What We May Be* (J. P. Tarcher), 74.

I will say something I have never said before—a compliment, a thank you, a declaration of love.

I will listen when I am prompted to speak.

I will slow my pattern of speech to ensure that I am saying what I most want to convey in the manner in which it will be most effectively received.

I will totally abstain from vulgar language and from using God's name irreverently.

I will counteract negative remarks with positive comments or with silence.

I will refrain both from being overly talkative and from moody silence.

I will extend a verbal greeting to someone who doesn't appeal to me.

I will say no when it is right to say no but easier to say yes.

I will say yes when it is right to say yes but easier to say no.

I will gently imagine beforehand my response to people I will be with.

I will read or recite aloud beautiful Scripture passages, prayers, or poetry.

I will speak tactfully from my own convictions, independently of what others think, say, or expect.

I will communicate to others what is deepest within me— feelings of anger, love, sadness.

This exercise can be adapted to any disordered area of behavior, by creating for oneself a list of actions that would positively strengthen one's will and facilitate change.

Closing

I close my prayer with a threefold conversation.

I turn to Mary who, with us, forms part of the community of all who have followed or do follow Christ. As mother of Jesus, she holds a special place in the communion of saints. In my own words, I ask her to obtain for me the gifts of

> a deep knowledge of my sinfulness and a hatred for sin
>
> an insight into the disorder in my life so that I may know how to refashion my life in the spirit of Jesus
>
> an awareness of whatever may distract and separate me from Christ, so that I may let go of all that deflects me from him

I turn to Jesus, begging him to ask the Father in his name for these same gifts for me.

I turn to God the Father, that he who loved us so much that he sent his only Son will give me these same graces.

I pray the Our Father.

Review of Prayer

I write in my journal the actions that I have chosen to strengthen my will. I write any feelings or insights that are motivating my choices.

Week Four, Day 3
Self-Encounter

....

JAMES 4:1–10

Those conflicts and disputes among you, where do they come from? Do they not come from your cravings that are at war within you? You want something and do not have it; so you commit murder. And you covet something and cannot obtain it; so you engage in disputes and conflicts. You do not have, because you do not ask. You ask and do not receive, because you ask wrongly, in order to spend what you get on your pleasures. Adulterers! Do you not know that friendship with the world is enmity with God? Therefore whoever wishes to be a friend of the world becomes an enemy of God. Or do you suppose that it is for nothing that the scripture says, "God yearns jealously for the spirit that he has made to dwell in us"? But he gives all the more grace; therefore it says, "God opposes the proud, but gives grace to the humble."

Submit yourselves therefore to God. Resist the devil, and he will flee from you. Draw near to God, and he will draw near to you. Cleanse your hands, you sinners, and purify your hearts, you double-minded. Lament and mourn and weep. Let your laughter be turned into mourning and your joy into dejection. Humble yourselves before the Lord, and he will exalt you.

Commentary

WE OFTEN WANT WHAT OTHERS have. We often envy the success of others. We are greedy, wanting more and more. We crave recognition and praise, wanting to be first and to be the best.

Our passions gone awry fight within us and wield heavy blows. Without God's help, we are unable to withstand their onslaught. Only by giving in to God, surrendering to the power of goodness, can we find peace.

Peace is not simply the absence of conflict and tension. Even if we could live this way, we would exist in a state of false harmony, lacking awareness and passively existing by either tolerating the conflict or denying it. We would be subject to, and live in fear of, inexplicable and unpredictable eruptions of anger within us.

The challenge is to face and confront our inner selves. Unless we are willing to put forth the prayer, reflection, and discipline necessary to grow in self-awareness, we will never discover the unconscious motivations behind our words and actions. We won't know why some particular things carry such a weight of importance to us. We will fail to ask ourselves the right question: "Do I see what I am doing?" (74, p. 163).

The inclination to be superior *to* and independent *of* others is common to all of us. In whatever arena we find ourselves, and however that superiority seeks expression, its name is pride. Given our propensity toward egotism, we need to be constantly alert, asking ourselves these questions:

What need triggers the underlying drive within me?

How does this action feed my desire to be self-sufficient and independent, not only of others but even of God?

How do the negative effects of my words and actions in the lives of others reveal or mirror my own area of sinfulness? What does their response say to me?

The answers to these questions will enable us to recognize our most authentic self, not only our potential for goodness but also our limitations, brokenness, and sinfulness. We will be led through this self-awareness into a deep mourning, as we are forced to accept the reality of the pain our actions have inflicted on others. The new level of consciousness will compel us to relinquish behaviors and values not based on our truest selves. Like idols, these values have deflected us from God. Unmasked, we see them for what they are—false gods. Do I see what I am doing and why I am doing it?

Our God is a God of blessing, and he yearns to be near us. Scripture gives us a poignant analogy of God's love, comparing it to the intimate love between husband and wife. For James, as for the Old Testament prophets, succumbing to the seduction of false gods was a matter not only of breaking the law but also of breaking God's heart. It was likened to the sin of adultery.

We belong to God. He loves us with a total love. He wants us to respond with our whole selves—body, mind, and heart (Matthew 22:37–38). Like a devoted spouse, God will not share us with other gods. "They made me jealous with what is no god, provoked me with their idols" (Deuteronomy 32:21).

Give in to God. To respond in love is to surrender; to surrender to the God of love is to pray always. To pray is to breathe deeply of the life-giving breath that God gave us at birth. Like life itself, prayer is an entry into a rhythm of love:

> the rhythm of God's nurturing love and our childlike dependency
>
> the rhythm of God's forgiving love and our tears

the rhythm of God's intimate love and our transparent receptivity

"Humble yourselves before the Lord, and he will exalt you."

Suggested Approach to Prayer

Daily Prayer Pattern
I quiet myself and relax in the presence of God.
I declare my dependence on God.

Grace
I draw near to God, asking for the gift to see clearly my own sinfulness and to be sincerely sorry.

Method: Prayer Word (refer to page 4)
"Draw near to God, and he will draw near to you"—I use these words as the basis for my prayer. As I breathe out, I will say softly, "The nearer I go to God," and breathing in, I will say, "the nearer he will come to me."

Closing
I close my prayer with a threefold conversation.

    I turn to Mary who, with us, forms part of the community of all who have followed or do follow Christ. As mother of Jesus, she holds a special place in the communion of saints. In my own words, I ask her to obtain for me the gifts of

    a deep knowledge of my sinfulness and a hatred for sin

an insight into the disorder in my life so that I may know how to refashion my life in the spirit of Jesus

an awareness of whatever may distract and separate me from Christ, so that I may let go of all that deflects me from him

I turn to Jesus, begging him to ask the Father in his name for these same gifts for me.

I turn to God the Father, that he who loved us so much that he sent his only Son will give me these same graces.

I pray the Our Father.

Review of Prayer

I write in my journal any feelings I had while praying.

Week Four, Day 4
False Treasure

LUKE 12:16–21

Then he told them a parable: "The land of a rich man produced abundantly. And he thought to himself, 'What should I do, for I have no place to store my crops?' Then he said, 'I will do this: I will pull down my barns and build larger ones, and there I will store all my grain and my goods. And I will say to my soul, Soul, you have ample goods laid up for many years; relax, eat, drink, be merry.' But God said to him, 'You fool! This very night your life is being demanded of you. And the things you have prepared, whose will they be?' So it is with those who store up treasures for themselves but are not rich toward God."

Commentary

ISN'T THIS A BORING STORY? All we hear from the farmer is what he has, how great his crop is, what he has done, and the good time he is going to have. Thank goodness that God speaks! God's words pierce through the false security of the rich man's plan.

God calls him a fool! Poor man, he had spent his entire life anxiously gathering, building, and storing. And now, just at the point when he could indulge himself, God tells him that he is bankrupt. The man is spiritually bankrupt, not rich at all in God's eyes.

The story about the rich man and God's response serves as an example for what our attitude should be toward material possessions. It cautions us not to place our security in them.

The relevance of the passage is strikingly apparent. In contemporary society there is an overwhelming tendency to identify ourselves and one another with what we have. The word *security* is often interpreted as meaning financial security. As a result, most of our energy and time are spent in the frantic pursuit of it.

The high incidence of stress-related illnesses in our culture lays bare the hidden truth of just how totally we have taken on this futile striving, collectively as well as individually. It is an unending, escalating struggle that, for some, literally ends in physical death. For others, life becomes a never-ending fixation on the self.

As strong a case as St. Luke presents, the intent is not to condemn material possessions. Nor can the passage be used to condone a life of laziness or irresponsible dependency. Neither can the meaning of this passage be limited to its interpretation as a warning in regard to our impending death and final judgment. There is a fuller meaning.

We are being alerted to the reality that our judgment is taking place now. Within our own hearts we are being judged by the Spirit. The judgment is tragic if we are guilty of neglecting and closing ourselves off to the kingdom that is already present within us and totally accessible at every moment.

The greatest sadness is not death; it is to have missed life. That is the tragedy of the rich man of this parable.

....

Therefore, since we are receiving a kingdom that cannot be shaken, let us give thanks, by which we offer to God an acceptable worship with reverence and awe.

Hebrews 12:28

....

Suggested Approach to Prayer

Daily Prayer Pattern
I quiet myself and relax in the presence of God.
I declare my dependence on God.

Grace
I ask for a growing awareness of my sinfulness and for a deepening sorrow.

Method
After recalling the parable, I listen carefully to the Holy Spirit speaking within me. I focus on a particular disorder, the one that emerges as the most apparent, basic, and insidious. I ask for the grace to recognize how this disorder is expressed by considering the following questions:

> What is it that I gather—riches, degrees, prestige?
>
> What have I built to house my treasures—roles, positions, buildings?
>
> What have I stored up as my security for the future—reputation, wealth, power, relationships?

Closing
I close my prayer with a threefold conversation.

I turn to Mary who, with us, forms part of the community of all who have followed or do follow Christ. As mother of Jesus, she holds a special place in the communion of saints. In my own words, I ask her to obtain for me the gifts of

a deep knowledge of my sinfulness and a hatred for sin

an insight into the disorder in my life so that I may know how to refashion my life in the spirit of Jesus

an awareness of whatever may distract and separate me from Christ, so that I may let go of all that deflects me from him

I turn to Jesus, begging him to ask the Father in his name for these same gifts for me.

I turn to God the Father, that he who loved us so much that he sent his only Son will give me these same graces.

I pray the Our Father.

Review of Prayer

I write in my journal my responses to the questions posed, as well as any feelings that surfaced during the period of prayer.

Week Four, Day 5
The Masks of Hypocrisy

MARK 7:1–23

Now when the Pharisees and some of the scribes who had come from Jerusalem gathered around him, they noticed that some of his disciples were eating with defiled hands, that is, without washing them. (For the Pharisees, and all the Jews, do not eat unless they thoroughly wash their hands, thus observing the tradition of the elders; and they do not eat anything from the market unless they wash it; and there are also many other traditions that they observe, the washing of cups, pots, and bronze kettles.) So the Pharisees and the scribes asked him, "Why do your disciples not live according to the tradition of the elders, but eat with defiled hands?" He said to them, "Isaiah prophesied rightly about you hypocrites, as it is written,

'This people honors me with their lips,
   but their hearts are far from me;
in vain do they worship me,
   teaching human precepts as doctrines.'

You abandon the commandment of God and hold to human tradition."

Then he said to them, "You have a fine way of rejecting the commandment of God in order to keep your tradition! For Moses said, 'Honor your father and your mother'; and, 'Whoever speaks evil of father or mother must surely die.' But you say that if anyone tells father or mother, 'Whatever support you might have had from me is Corban' (that is, an offering to God)—then you no longer permit doing anything for a father or mother, thus making void the word of God through your tradition that you have handed on. And you do many things like this."

Then he called the crowd again and said to them, "Listen to me, all of you, and understand: there is nothing outside a person that by going in can defile, but the things that come out are what defile."

When he had left the crowd and entered the house, his disciples asked him about the parable. He said to them, "Then do you also fail to understand? Do you not see that whatever goes into a person from outside cannot defile, since it enters, not the heart but the stomach, and goes out into the sewer?" (Thus he declared all foods clean.) And he said, "It is what comes out of a person that defiles. For it is from within, from the human heart, that evil intentions come: fornication, theft, murder, adultery, avarice, wickedness, deceit, licentiousness, envy, slander, pride, folly. All these evil things come from within, and they defile a person."

Commentary

IN MARK 7, WE FIND some of the most revolutionary teachings in the New Testament. With prophetic insight, Jesus spoke out against the external practices that had been adopted and endorsed as the essence of religious worship. By word and example, Jesus nullified the system of cultic purity, which was based on a concept of what was clean and unclean.

Tragically, the people had lost sight of the hope and freedom offered to them through the Mosaic covenant. Subject to the oppressive leadership of the scribes and Pharisees, they labored under an intolerable weight of rules and regulations.

The essential difference between the teachings of Jesus and the mentality of the Pharisees is made clear in this passage. The Pharisees were a lay group who, historically, stood in opposition to the Jewish priestly class. The name *Pharisee* means "separate"; by their fanaticism for ritual and law, the Pharisees had set themselves apart from the rest of society. In their isolation, their attitude tended toward comparison and inflated superiority.

Adherence to the law and tradition was meticulous. Every letter of the law was compulsively obeyed. The pitfall was that what began historically as a sincere effort to renew Judaic faith resulted in an obsessive exaggeration of law. Ironically, the law itself became an obstacle to inner renewal. So much happened externally that nothing took place interiorly. Gradually, external practices of the law began to be used as an escape from the deeper obligation and summons of God's command to love:

You shall love the LORD *your God with all your heart, and with all your soul, and with all your might. Keep these words . . . in your heart.*

DEUTERONOMY 6:5–6

Appalled by these excessive practices, Jesus did not spare the Pharisees. He severely condemned the hypocrisy perpetrated by their excesses. Hypocrisy is the wearing of a mask, and the Pharisees were wearing masks to play roles of people they wanted to be. This was totally unacceptable to Jesus. Many of the Pharisees, motivated by self-interest and the desire to make a good impression, abused their religious authority and manipulated the sincerity of the people to serve their own advancement.

In this passage, Jesus harshly criticized and accused the Pharisees of hypocrisy in two separate situations: the compulsiveness of ritual cleansing, and the clever deception of practices such as *corban*.

The heated exchange began when the Pharisees challenged Jesus because his disciples did not observe the tradition of washing their hands before eating. Jesus and the disciples were confronted with long-standing traditions that had taken on the force of law. Orally handed down from generation to generation, these rigid traditions, known as the *Halakak*, were an elaborate body of rules and regulations intended to govern every conceivable action and circumstance.

The directives regulating the ceremonial cleansing of hands and vessels reached absurd proportions. Hands had to be cleansed in a particular manner, and the specific methods for cleansing vessels were determined by the shape, the material, and the function of the container.

Angered by the Pharisees' efforts to impose their sterile customs on his disciples, Jesus lashed out and called them hypocrites. He pierced the protective shield of their self-righteousness by presenting them with the contradictory and contemptible reality of their situation. The accusation that Isaiah had leveled at Israel centuries earlier, Jesus now applied to the Pharisees:

This people honors me with their lips, but their hearts are far from me; in vain do they worship me, teaching human precepts as doctrines.

MARK 7:6–7

With unerring accuracy and biting sarcasm, Jesus delivered judgment: "You have a fine way of rejecting the commandment of God in order to keep your tradition!"

His second charge involved a concrete example of their dubious ingenuity. It addressed the unjust and popular practice of *corban*. Originally, corban was a practice of offering one's gifts to God—the gifts themselves were called corban. By the time of Jesus, the practice of corban had fallen into abuse. The Pharisees used it to serve their own interests and to escape real obligations, even to the point of neglecting the care of their aging parents.

Whatever was proclaimed corban could not legally be used for other purposes; it belonged to God. A son might say, "I cannot help you because all my money is promised to God." With that formal assertion, the money was no longer available for the care of his parents, even if later he were to retract his promise.

Once again Jesus called on their deeper tradition to witness in the case against the Pharisees. He confronted them with the fundamental teaching of Moses: "Honor your father and your mother" and "Whoever speaks evil of father or mother must surely die."

But Jesus was not yet finished. He went on to say that this was only one case among many in which they had justified their behavior and indulged their need for prestige and control. The price they had paid for this blatant abuse of God's law was the negation of their own innermost spirit: God's word for them had become null and void. A phenomenal tragedy—they were spiritually blind leaders!

Jesus, moved with compassion, turned to address all the people, inviting them to listen and understand. The invitation to "all of you" indicated the universality of Jesus' message and the death of spiritual elitism. The instruction to "understand" signified the importance of the message that followed: nothing that goes into a person from outside can make him unclean; it is the things that come out of a person that make him unclean. The message was not only important; it was surprising and new!

In one radical declaration, Jesus effectively shattered the rigid moral and ethical structure, which was based on distinction of cleanness and uncleanness. Things in themselves were declared neither clean nor unclean, neither good nor bad. By this declaration Jesus rejected *superfluous externals*. Traditions, prescriptions, rules, and rituals should not substitute for religious experience.

Much to Jesus' chagrin, the disciples did not understand this teaching. He took them aside and privately explained it further. The core of his message was that we must discover the ultimate rule of love within ourselves. In the end, we must go beyond external rules. Jesus calls on each person to enter the depths of his or her own heart and consciousness and discover there the authentic truth that goes beyond the strictures of the law. The spiritual quality, the "cleanness" of any outward expression—by word or action—is in proportion to that person's attentiveness to God's Spirit within him or her.

Suggested Approach to Prayer

Daily Prayer Pattern

I quiet myself and relax in the presence of God.
I declare my dependence on God.

Grace

I ask to deepen the awareness of my sinfulness and for a growing sorrow.

Method

Jesus had harsh words for *hypocrites*, a word whose root meaning referred to those who "wear a mask" as actors did in ancient times, to represent the role they were playing.

I stand before Jesus. He looks at me. I look into his eyes, and there, what do I see reflected?

What are the roles I play? The one who is always right? The one who is in control?

Do I smile outwardly while carrying a grudge?

I look into the eyes of Jesus as into a mirror and allow my masks to appear.

I listen to the words Jesus addressed to the Pharisees as if he were speaking directly to me. What do I learn about myself from the feelings and images his words arouse in me?

Closing

I close my prayer with a threefold conversation.

I turn to Mary who, with us, forms part of the community of all who have followed or do follow Christ. As mother of Jesus, she holds a special place in the communion of saints. In my own words, I ask her to obtain for me the gifts of

> a deep knowledge of my sinfulness and a hatred for sin
>
> an insight into the disorder in my life so that I may know how to refashion my life in the spirit of Jesus

an awareness of whatever may distract and separate me from Christ, so that I may let go of all that deflects me from him

I turn to Jesus, begging him to ask the Father in his name for these same gifts for me.

I turn to God the Father, that he who loved us so much that he sent his only Son will give me these same graces.

I pray the Our Father.

Review of Prayer

I write in my journal any feelings that were elicited as I listened to Jesus speak to me.

Week Four, Day 6

Pharisee or Tax Collector?

....

LUKE 18:9–14

He also told this parable to some who trusted in themselves that they were righteous and regarded others with contempt: "Two men went up to the temple to pray, one a Pharisee and the other a tax collector. The Pharisee, standing by himself, was praying thus, 'God, I thank you that I am not like other people: thieves, rogues, adulterers, or even like this tax collector. I fast twice a week; I give a tenth of all my income.' But the tax collector, standing far off, would not even look up to heaven, but was beating his breast and saying, 'God, be merciful to me, a sinner!' I tell you, this man went down to his home justified rather than the other; for all who exalt themselves will be humbled, but all who humble themselves will be exalted."

Commentary

THE PHARISEE OR THE TAX collector—who are you? Contrary to our tendency to identify with one or the other, the greater truth is that within each of us are the dispositions and attitudes of both.

There is something about the Pharisee that makes us cringe! In the parable, the Pharisee is depicted as superior and pompous. The Pharisees were faithful to the law. They fasted, they prayed, they paid tithes on all they earned. Externally and publicly they observed all the prescribed religious laws. The Pharisee of the parable was no exception.

But how was his prayer? In one translation of this passage, the Pharisee is described as praying *to* himself. This is amusing, as a closer look discloses that he literally did pray to *himself!* What began as thanksgiving to God regressed to a self-congratulatory litany. Standing with arms extended, filled with overconfidence, he used the forum of the temple to fulfill his own need for recognition. What externally appeared as prayer was, in fact, no prayer at all.

The stance and expression of the tax collector was a startling contrast to that of the Pharisee. The tax collector took his place at a distance, his head bowed, his eyes cast down as he pleaded for mercy. His clenched fist against his heart expressed the intensity of his inner anguish. The original text indicates that the tax collector did not think of himself as simply a sinner, but as *the* sinner. He had an acute awareness of the depth and extent of his personal sinfulness, of the fraud, the duplicity, the cheating that had shaped his life as a public servant. With the psalmist he could pray:

For I know my transgressions,
    and my sin is ever before me.
Against you, you alone, have I sinned.

PSALM 51:3–4

In contrast to the prayer of the Pharisee, the prayer of the tax collector was humble. He had searched his heart, and he had discovered his guilt. In helplessness he threw himself on God's compassionate love and mercy. It was at the moment of truth and surrender that the tax collector was lifted up.

The difference between the Pharisee and the tax collector was sustained to the end of the story. In his self-exultation, the

Pharisee went away empty. In contrast, by submitting himself to God's mercy and forgiveness, the tax collector was freed from the binding effects of his sins. His confession of guilt opened to him the deeper reality of himself; it prepared the way for his mature and moral completeness in Christ. "[*He*] *went down to his home justified.*"

Jesus closes his teaching simply and directly: whoever exalts himself will be humbled and whoever humbles himself will be exalted.

Suggested Approach to Prayer

Daily Prayer Pattern

I quiet myself and relax in the presence of God.

I declare my dependence on God.

Grace

I ask for the grace to deepen the awareness of my sinfulness and for a growing sorrow.

Method: Contemplation

I imagine myself in the temple. I see the temple in great detail, becoming aware of the crowd of worshippers.

Recognizing that there is within me both the Pharisee and the tax collector, I first assume the role of the Pharisee. I take the position and interior stance of prayer that was his. I pray a similar prayer of superiority that reflects my own attitudes and tendencies toward comparison.

Next, I assume the role, position, and interior stance of the tax collector. I pray as he prayed, expressing sorrow and begging God's mercy for my sins.

At the end of my contemplation of the Pharisee and the tax collector, I ask myself these questions:

What feeling arose within me?

What did I learn about myself—about my attitudes, my areas of sinfulness, and the depth of my sorrow?

Then I listen and watch Jesus as he prays the Our Father.

Closing

I close my prayer with a threefold conversation.

I turn to Mary who, with us, forms part of the community of all who have followed or do follow Christ. As mother of Jesus, she holds a special place in the communion of saints. In my own words, I ask her to obtain for me the gifts of

a deep knowledge of my sinfulness and a hatred for sin

an insight into the disorder in my life so that I may know how to refashion my life in the spirit of Jesus

an awareness of whatever may distract and separate me from Christ, so that I may let go of all that deflects me from him

I turn to Jesus, begging him to ask the Father in his name for these same gifts from me.

I turn to God the Father, that he who loved us so much that he sent his only Son will give me these same graces.

I pray the Our Father.

Review of Prayer

I write in my journal the feelings, experiences, and insights that occurred during this period of prayer.

Week Five, Day 1

Repetition

....

Suggested Approach to Prayer

Daily Prayer Pattern

I quiet myself and relax in the presence of God.

I declare my dependence on God.

Grace

I ask for a growing awareness of the root of my sinful disorders and for a deepening sorrow.

Method: Repetition

In preparation, I review my previous prayer periods by reading my journal since the last repetition day. I select for my repetition the period of prayer in which I was most deeply moved or the one in which I experienced dryness or a lack of emotional response. I use the method with which I approached the passage initially. I open myself to hear again God's word to me in that particular passage.

Review of Prayer

I write in my journal any feelings, experiences, or insights that have surfaced in this second "listening."

Part Four

God's Merciful Forgiveness

Week Five, Day 2

The Forgiving Father

LUKE 15:11–32

Then Jesus said, "There was a man who had two sons. The younger of them said to his father, 'Father, give me the share of the property that will belong to me.' So he divided his property between them. A few days later the younger son gathered all he had and traveled to a distant country, and there he squandered his property in dissolute living.

"When he had spent everything, a severe famine took place throughout that country, and he began to be in need. So he went and hired himself out to one of the citizens of that country, who sent him to his fields to feed the pigs. He would gladly have filled himself with the pods that the pigs were eating; and no one gave him anything. But when he came to himself he said, 'How many of my father's hired hands have bread enough and to spare, but here I am dying of hunger! I will get up and go to my father, and I will say to him, "Father, I have sinned against heaven and before you; I am no longer worthy to be called your son; treat me like one of your hired hands."' So he set off and went to his father. But while he was still far off, his father saw him and was filled with compassion; he ran and put his arms around him and kissed him. Then the son said to him, 'Father, I have sinned against heaven and before you; I am no longer worthy to be called your son.' But the father said to his slaves, 'Quickly, bring out a robe—the best one—and put it on him; put a ring on his finger and sandals on his feet. And get the fatted calf and kill it, and let us eat and celebrate; for this son of mine was dead and is alive again; he was lost and is found!' And they began to celebrate.

"Now his elder son was in the field; and when he came and approached the house, he heard music and dancing. He called one of the slaves and asked what was going on. He replied, 'Your brother has come, and your father has killed the fatted calf, because he has got him back safe and sound.' Then he became angry and refused to go in. His father came out and began to plead with him. But he answered his father, 'Listen! For all these years I have been working like a slave for you, and I have never disobeyed your command; yet you have never given me even a young goat so that I might celebrate with my friends. But when this son of yours came back, who has devoured your property with prostitutes, you killed the fatted calf for him!' Then the father said to him, 'Son, you are always with me, and all that is mine is yours. But we had to celebrate and rejoice, because this brother of yours was dead and has come to life; he was lost and has been found.'"

Commentary

THIS IS SURELY ONE OF the most beautiful stories ever written! It has been celebrated on stage, in art and music, and most significantly, it has been relived in countless lives and families. Luke has so exquisitely rendered the feelings of the father and his sons that we are immediately drawn into the drama of this very human situation.

This is the story of a father who had two sons. He "lost them both, one in a foreign country, the other behind a barricade of self-righteousness" (16, p. 182). Popularly known as the parable of the prodigal son, a more appropriate title might be the parable of the forgiving father, because the focus of the story is primarily on the father's love and mercy toward his sons.

One can imagine the father's feelings when the younger son requested his inheritance—what would belong to him when his father died. Although it was not uncommon to see an estate divided among heirs before death, it seemed as if the younger son could not wait for his father to die.

As he watched his son go down the road, carrying "all he had," the father must have been filled with apprehension for him. Then his worst fears were realized! The son lavishly spent and wasted his father's gift until he was reduced to abject poverty. He was hungry; he was homeless; he was alone.

He had sunk to what, for a Jew, was the lowest possible level, for he was reduced to caring for the pigs of a Gentile landowner. For the Jews, the pig was considered the most unclean of all animals, and to be employed by a Gentile was to be under the influence and control of one who worshipped foreign gods. Finally, at the point of death—"I am dying of hunger"—he came to his senses and was filled with the desire to return home.

Even in the moment of deepest despair, his father's love was active in his memories. The father's deep longing for his son was present within the son's burning desire to return home. Though distant, father and son were united in love and yearning for each other—one calling, one responding.

The father received his son; he kissed him tenderly. The son began his carefully rehearsed admission of guilt. He said, "I have sinned against heaven and before you. I am no longer worthy to be called your son."

He was interrupted by his father's uncontained joy. In the embrace of his father, the son was welcomed, forgiven, and restored to full sonship. His father honored him with a fine robe to cover his nakedness. He received from his father a ring, which signified the reinstatement of his authority as a son in his father's house. The sandals that were placed on his feet were further indication that he was not a slave, because only free people wore shoes. The son had been lost and found. Now he knew what it meant to be his father's son. He was home! The father was overjoyed: "My son has come to life; let the celebration begin!"

No sooner had the music and dancing begun than the other, older son stormed in and confronted their father. However disappointed the father may have been by the older son's resentment and ill will, he had the wisdom not to take sides. He may have sensed that the older son was suffering an alienation of his own. The older son's attitudes had distanced him from his brother to such an extent that he referred to him not as "my brother" but as "this son of yours." His self-righteous attitudes had prevented him from entering into a loving relationship, not only with his brother but also with his father. The elder son, too, was lost; he was lost in a foreign land of his own making.

The father responded as he had with his younger son. He was compassionate. He did not ridicule his son, but rebuked him gently. "You are always with me, and all that is mine is yours." All the father was able to do was invite the son to confront his negativity, accept his own position, and enter into the joy of his brother's return.

As sons and daughters of our Father, we are invited to claim the reality of our inheritance as sons and daughters of a loving and merciful God. The banquet is prepared. Will you enter into the joy of your Father?

Suggested Approach to Prayer

Daily Prayer Pattern

I quiet myself and relax in the presence of God.
I declare my dependence on God.

Grace

I ask for a deepening awareness of my sinfulness and a growing sorrow.

Method: Contemplation

I enter this passage by allowing the story to unfold within me. I invite one of the sons to come forward. I assume his role and relive it in my imagination, observing in detail his actions and words.

If I choose the younger son, I imagine requesting my inheritance, leaving home, and squandering the money. If I choose the elder son, I imagine my situation, my resentment toward my brother, the conversation with my father, and his invitation. I follow the story to its completion.

Closing

I close my prayer with a threefold conversation.

I turn to Mary who, with us, forms part of the community of all who have followed or do follow Christ. As mother of Jesus, she holds a special place in the communion of saints. In my own words, I ask her to obtain for me the gifts of

a deep knowledge of my sinfulness and a hatred for sin

an insight into the disorder in my life so that I may know how to refashion my life in the spirit of Jesus

an awareness of whatever may distract and separate me from Christ, so that I may let go of all that deflects me from him

I turn to Jesus, begging him to ask the Father in his name for these same gifts for me.

I turn to God the Father, that he who loved us so much that he sent his only Son will give me these same graces.

I pray the Our Father.

Review of Prayer

I write in my journal any feelings, experiences, or insights that surfaced during this period of prayer. I take special note of those that relate to my response to the Father.

Week Five, Day 3

Coming Home

....

Reread Luke 15:11–32.

Commentary

THE STORY OF THE FORGIVING father and the two sons touches the center of each of us. In a sense, we have within us both sons. We are at once the younger, pleasure-seeking son and the older, duty-bound, overly responsible son. One of the two is dominant and most easily identifiable. The other, however, is nonetheless present and seeks to express himself. Like an ignored child, the denied son reacts negatively, trying to get our attention.

If a person identifies primarily with the elder, duty-bound son, his sinfulness will likely be an exaggeration of conscientiousness, concern for what others think, and a need to be accepted and approved. The pleasure-seeking son who is denied will likely make himself known in sullen moodiness, where all joy will be absent, spontaneity squelched, and sensitivity to others withheld.

In contrast, if that same person identifies primarily with the younger, pleasure-seeking son, his sinfulness will likely be in preoccupation with self- and overindulgence. The denied son will probably make himself known by subtly undermining the person's self-esteem; as a consequence, the individual may become a slave to addictions or binges of compulsive rituals such as food, drink, sex, or spending.

The danger for us, as it was for the sons in the story, is an overidentification with either dimension. Although it is important for us to recognize our preferred "son," the deeper challenge is to reconcile within ourselves both dimensions. Like the prodigal son, we need to come to our senses, to discover our true selves. There is within us a wonderful potential, more than we could dream of or imagine. We are invited to claim the gifts each son has to offer us. The elder son holds out for us the strength of stability, perseverance, and faithfulness, and the younger son is offering us the joys of spontaneity, sensitivity, and creativity.

We are called to come home to claim our gifts. For us, as for the prodigal son, to come home means to return to our Father. It is there, in the embrace of his love, that we are unconditionally accepted and our sins are forgiven. All that is fragmented within us is reconciled, and we experience new life.

But God, who is rich in mercy, out of the great love with which he loved us even when we were dead through our trespasses, made us alive together with Christ.

EPHESIANS 2:4–5

Our way to union, within ourselves and with God, is Jesus. Paul's letter to the Ephesians (2:13–19) reads like a commentary on this parable:

But now in Christ Jesus you who once were far off have been brought near by the blood of Christ. For he is our peace; in his flesh he has made both groups into one and has broken down the dividing wall, that is, the hostility between us. He has abolished the law with its commandments and ordinances, so that he might create in himself one new humanity in place of the two, thus making peace, and might reconcile both groups to God in one body through the cross, thus putting to death that hostility through it. So he came and proclaimed peace to you who were far off and peace to those who were near; for through him both of us have access in one Spirit to the Father. So then you are no longer strangers and aliens, but you are citizens with the saints and also members of the household of God.

Suggested Approach to Prayer

Daily Prayer Pattern
I quiet myself and relax in the presence of God.
I declare my dependence on God.

Grace
I ask for a deepening awareness of my sinfulness and for a growing sorrow.

Method
I meditatively reread Paul's letter to the Ephesians (2:4–5, 13–19). I read it as a letter addressed personally to me. I respond by writing a letter to God, my Father.

I thank God for the gifts of each "son" that lives in me, and what it is about each one that I love.

I beg God to *help me*, by sending the living Spirit of Jesus to help me reconcile and integrate these two wonderful, yet conflicting dimensions within myself.

I proclaim my love for God, giving expression to my wish to accept fully all he intends for me, and to do what he requires to bring it to fullness.

I tell God that I am sorry for the many times I have succumbed to the weakness and seductions of each dimension, thereby rejecting his love. I share with God the specific ways in which this has happened.

I close my letter by letting my heart speak of my deep desire to make God's heart my home. I ask for the strength and wisdom of his love to protect me, moment to moment, from every evil and temptation.

Closing

I close my prayer with a threefold conversation.

I turn to Mary who, with us, forms part of the community of all who have followed or do follow Christ. As mother of Jesus, she holds a special place in the communion of saints. In my own words, I ask her to obtain for me the gifts of

deep knowledge of my sinfulness and a hatred for sin

an insight into the disorder in my life so that I may know how to refashion my life in the spirit of Jesus

an awareness of whatever may distract and separate me from Christ, so that I may let go of all that deflects me from him

I turn to Jesus, begging him to ask the Father in his name for these same gifts for me.

I turn to God the Father, that he who loved us so much that he sent his only Son will give me these same graces.

I pray the Our Father.

Review of Prayer

I write in my journal the most prominent feelings I experienced while writing the letter to God.

Part Five

A Glimpse
of Hell

Week Five, Day 4

The Final Loss

....

Hebrews 10:26–29

For if we willfully persist in sin after having received the knowledge of the truth, there no longer remains a sacrifice for sins, but a fearful prospect of judgment, and a fury of fire that will consume the adversaries. Anyone who has violated the law of Moses dies without mercy "on the testimony of two or three witnesses." How much worse punishment do you think will be deserved by those who have spurned the Son of God, profaned the blood of the covenant by which they were sanctified, and outraged the Spirit of grace?

Commentary

IT IS ONE THING TO sin when one is ignorant; it is quite another to choose to sin, deliberately and maliciously. As the biblical commentator William Barclay has said, "The greater the knowledge, the greater the sin" (4, p. 124). And the greater the sin, the greater the punishment.

The knowledge that the author of Hebrews is addressing is the inner, experiential heart knowledge that we have of Jesus. It is the knowledge received by those who had been called, initiated, and baptized into the Christian community.

The writer is horrified at the thought that those who know Jesus could reject him. How could one who had been freed from the burden of guilt, one who had received the gift of the Spirit, one who had been instructed by the words of Jesus and enjoyed the fellowship of communion, possibly reject Christ?

How could that person spurn such love? How could he or she treat and dismiss as nothing the death through which Jesus offered fullness of life? How could he or she "outrage the Spirit"? Such a person would be like a field that had been watered and blessed with good crops, and then later grew only brambles and thistles. It will end by being abandoned and cursed; "its end is to be burned over" (Hebrews 6:8).

The greater the sin, the greater is the punishment. The price to be paid for the deliberate and absolute rejection of God's love defies imagination. In this passage it is described as *"a fury of fire that will consume the adversaries."*

Upon reading those words, medieval depictions of hell come to mind. In turn, these call up archetypal images of sinners writhing in pain, of putrid smells of sulfur and smoke, of isolation, and of unending darkness.

This common conception of hell was originally drawn from numerous biblical references to judgment and punishment. In the Old Testament, though, the word *hell* was not used; Gehenna, the Valley of Death, was designated as the place where the dead bodies of those who rebelled against Yahweh would lie. Referring to it, Isaiah (66:24) said:

And they shall go out and look at the dead bodies of the people who have rebelled against me; for their worm shall not die, their fire shall not be quenched, and they shall be an abhorrence to all flesh.

In the New Testament, Gehenna, the place of punishment, was described as the place where the wicked, body and soul, are destroyed (Matthew 10:28). It was "the lake of fire that burns with sulfur" (Revelation 19:20), where those punished are salted with fire (Mark 9:49), and are "tormented day and night forever and ever" (Revelation 20:10). It is the domain of darkness and misery, of "weeping and gnashing of teeth" (Matthew 8:12). It is separated from this life by a "great chasm" (Luke 16:26).

In using these images in his teaching and parables, Jesus attempted to convey to his followers the seriousness of sin and its tragic consequences. These strong and vivid images are meant to stimulate and elicit, by way of imagination, a totally human and integrated response of senses and intellect.

We can try to relate to the reality of hell by imagining a person who is in total darkness and thereby deprived of all light, both physical and intellectual. He or she would be terrified, groping, and confused. In the darkness, the senses would take on an extraordinary acuteness. The intense quiet might be experienced as thunderous, the smell as musty, the taste like that of fungus, and the feel as that of a clammy mist. These imagined sense experiences of the horror of hell can fill us with utter abhorrence, fear, and repulsion at the prospect of such an eventuality for ourselves, just as it might have for Jesus' listeners.

Yet, however vivid the imaginative experience of hell, it would be merely a shadow of its devastating reality. For, as one writer points out, hell is not a place, or even a state of being, but a "condition of non-being" (45, p. 1152).

Everything is at stake—all of who we are and all of who God intends us to be! Our total integrity rests on our moment-to-moment choosing. The choice is for or against God. To reject

God totally—to choose sin and to allow that sin to be lived in its entirety—would be to lose everything. We would be totally alienated, not only from God but also from our very selves. We would no longer *be*.

The church teaches that no one is predestined to go to hell. It requires a willful turning away from God and a persistence to remain that way until the end of life. However, we do carry in our human frailty the seeds of such destruction. The realization of this possibility can only cause one to fear—to have a healthy fear—of ourselves and our capability for evil.

Suggested Approach to Prayer

Daily Prayer Pattern

I quiet myself and relax in the presence of God.
I declare my dependence on God.

Grace

I ask for a sense of the loss that is the essence of hell so that, in the event that I would lose the vision of God's love, the fear of hell would keep me from sin.

Method

In my imagination, I enter into the experience of hell. I let myself become aware of the absolute finality, confinement, and shallowness of hell as opposed to the length, breadth, height, and depth of Christ's love.

Using the New Testament images quoted in the commentary, I further enter into the experience of hell with my whole being, using in turn each of my five senses:

seeing the fires

hearing the wailing and gnashing of teeth

smelling the smoke and sulfur

tasting the bitterness

touching the burning coals

Closing

"Once I have let the awfulness of this experience sink deep within me, I begin to talk to Christ our Lord about it. I talk to him about all the people who have lived—the many who have lived before his coming and who deliberately closed in upon themselves and chose such a hell for all eternity, the many who walked with him in his own country and who rejected his call to love, the many who still keep rejecting the call to love and remain locked in their own chosen hell.

"I give thanks to Jesus that he has not put an end to my life and allowed me to fall into any of these groups. All I can do is to give thanks to him that up to this very moment, he has shown himself so loving and merciful to me" (28, p. 47).

I close with the Our Father.

Review of Prayer

I write in my journal the "vision" of hell that I experienced in my imagination. I write the feelings that most gripped me.

Week Five, Day 5
The Final Loss, Part 2

....

Reread Hebrews 10:26–29 and its commentary on pages 144–147.

Suggested Approach to Prayer

Daily Prayer Pattern

I quiet myself and relax in the presence of God.
I declare my dependence on God.

Grace

I ask for a sense of the loss that is the essence of hell so that, in the event that I would lose the vision of God's love, the fear of hell would keep me from sin.

Method

In my imagination, I enter the experience of hell. I become aware of one of my most basic disorders, the area in which I am most prone to sin.

I consider how I have succumbed to this sin in the past. I allow myself to imagine what would happen if I were to give free and complete reign to that sin. I imagine in detail all the ramifications: its effects on those I love, on the community I live in, on myself.

Using each of my five senses, I further enter into the hell I could cause by this sin:

I will see it.

I will hear it.

I will smell it.

I will taste it.

I will touch it.

I will let the seriousness, the pain, and the sorrow for my sinfulness sink deeply into me.

Closing

"Once I have let the awfulness of this experience sink deep within me, I begin to talk to Christ our Lord about it. I talk to him about all the people who have lived—the many who have lived before his coming and who deliberately closed in upon themselves and chose such a hell for all eternity, the many who walked with him in his own country and who rejected his call to love, the many who still keep rejecting the call to love and remain locked in their own chosen hell.

"I give thanks to Jesus that he has not put an end to my life and allowed me to fall into any of these groups. All I can do is to give thanks to him that up to this very moment, he has shown himself so loving and merciful to me" (28, p. 47).

I close with the Our Father.

Review of Prayer

I write in my journal the sorrow I experienced for my sinfulness.

Week Five, Day 6
The Ultimate Collapse

....

REVELATION 18:2, 21–23

"Fallen, fallen is Babylon the great!
    It has become a dwelling place of demons,
a haunt of every foul spirit,
    a haunt of every foul bird,
    a haunt of every foul and hateful beast."

Then a mighty angel took up a stone like a great millstone and threw it into the sea, saying,

"With such violence Babylon the great city
    will be thrown down,
    and will be found no more;
and the sound of harpists and minstrels and of flutists and
        trumpeters
    will be heard in you no more;
and an artisan of any trade
    will be found in you no more;
and the sound of the millstone
    will be heard in you no more;
and the light of a lamp
    will shine in you no more;
and the voice of bridegroom and bride
    will be heard in you no more."

Commentary

THERE ONCE WAS A SMALL band of people who lived together harmoniously. Individually and together, they had a vision and a task: to create. So powerful was the vision that it was as if they had been mysteriously chosen.

Together they built a small city and in the center constructed a beautiful temple in which to worship the God of their joy. The light that burned in the sanctuary could be seen from every home in the city.

Gregarious and fun loving, the people took advantage of every possible occasion to celebrate. They loved to sing and dance. Weddings were three-day affairs. Every day they went eagerly to their task of creating and were extraordinarily successful. Not only were their creations appreciated and sought throughout the known world, but their style of community was emulated by many in the hopes that they, too, might experience the release of such creative power.

As the years went by, the reputation and fame of the community grew. More and more people came to purchase its works of art. As the orders began to accumulate, the artists experienced pressure from having to produce so much. No longer did they welcome each new day. By nightfall, they were too tired to pray or to enjoy one another.

The people began to be preoccupied with the money from the escalating sales of their art. The money grew to such proportions that, finding no place large enough in which to store and guard it, they built a bank at each corner of the city. These buildings rose like four giant pillars.

In their newfound fame and affluence, the people became very possessive of their unique gift of creativity. They were unwilling to share the secrets of their craft, even among themselves. They rationalized that the power of creativity might be dissipated through sharing.

Filled with fear, they created an army and prepared themselves for an imagined attack from those who might covet their riches. No longer trustful, the people began to do things they would not have considered in the early days. They constructed a wall with gates that were kept locked, even during daylight. Although they had telephones, they were not connected with the outside world. Visitors from the outside became progressively rarer and unwelcome. Of those few who chose to leave, stories circulated that they had met their death beyond the gates.

Something was happening to the people, and it became ever more obvious. The rooms in which the people created their artwork changed from centers of exhilaration to places of tomblike silence. Creations were churned out, one after another, but each one looked exactly like the preceding one. If per chance someone with bright eyes laughingly produced a new design, it was quickly squelched as a deformation. There was no freshness, no vitality. The power was gone.

Slowly through the years, the community grew increasingly isolated from the outside world—and increasingly divided within its own world. Chaos had come (Isaiah 34:11). Marriages were few and always without festivity (Jeremiah 7:34). Births were infrequent. The spirit of the people had died. The light in the temple had long since flickered out (Jeremiah 25:10). The building itself was in shambles (Ezekiel 26:12) and had become a shelter for mice and owls (Isaiah 34:11). Years later, people remembered the community and went into the wilderness in search for it. They looked in vain (Ezekiel 26:21).

This story illustrates the spiritual collapse of an entire community of people. Their withdrawal, self-preoccupation, and mistrust of others resulted in the loss of creativity, joy, and spirit. Within the hell of their own making, they ceased to be.

In the book of Revelation, we find a description of the collapse of the city of Babylon. Because Revelation was addressed to the Christian community during a time of persecution, it is filled with symbolic images that would have been understandable only to the initiated members.

On one level of meaning, Babylon signified Rome, whose emperor ruled the known world. As the capital of the ancient land of Jewish exile, Babylon came to be identified with all that was opposed to Yahweh. It was thought of as an evil, immoral city. Its collapse and fall were seen by the Hebrew prophets as signs of God's judgment and punishment.

The depth of its collapse was equaled only by the height of its former accomplishments and creativity. Even today, Babylon is synonymous with art and architecture. The wanton deterioration of this once beautiful and prominent center of culture was tragic.

In its glory, Babylon had a highly developed and humane system of government. The Babylonians were responsible for making significant advances in the areas of science, astrology, and mathematics. Artifacts from that period give evidence of a highly skilled craftsmanship.

One of the most valuable contributions of the Babylonians to modern civilization was that they committed to writing the myths, hymns, and history of their times. These songs and stories provide a link between Babylon and early Judaic traditions and beliefs. Such literary treasures have made a significant impact on our contemporary understanding of Scripture and its historical roots.

Ironically, the very gifts that brought the Babylonians to such an extraordinary level of civilization influenced their downfall. In spite of the idealism expressed in some of the Babylonian hymns and other writings, Babylon's religion had little moral impact. Emphasizing this world and its goods, it was an undemanding and superficial religion that was conducive to superstitious practices.

For the prophets of Judah, the fall of Babylon was never simply a matter of external political and economic forces. It was the logical consequence of a people materially unrestrained, morally undisciplined, and religiously sterile.

And Babylon, the glory of kingdoms,
    the splendor and pride of the Chaldeans,
will be like Sodom and Gomorrah
    when God overthrew them.
It will never be inhabited
    or lived in for all generations;
Arabs will not pitch their tents there,
    shepherds will not make their flocks lie down there.
But wild animals will lie down there,
    and its houses will be full of howling creatures.

ISAIAH 13:19–21

The book of Revelation draws on the prophets in its bitter criticism of the sinfulness of the Roman Empire. The judgment of such sinfulness is described in words that deeply penetrate our human consciousness and cause us to respond with repulsion and fear. That response is none other than that which we experience when, in our more lucid moments, we contemplate our world in *its* sinfulness and our personal share in it.

Suggested Approach to Prayer

Daily Prayer Pattern
I quiet myself and relax in the presence of God.
I declare my dependence on God.

Grace
I ask for a sense of the loss that is the essence of hell so that, in the event that I would lose the vision of God's love, the fear of hell would keep me from sin.

Method
As I enter this time of prayer, I become aware of the pain of loss that accompanies all sin, and the incredible sin that inflicts humanity.

I take into my hands a real or imagined globe of the earth. Turning it gently and slowly in my hands, I bring to mind and heart all the sins of the people of the earth.

I consider the greed that has exploited the less fortunate and those without economic or political power; the violence that has resulted in rape, abuse, and murder; the irreverence that has torn families apart and split churches; the corruption that has ruined governments; the unnecessary consumption that has polluted our air and water.

I continue in this matter to consider the horror of the sins that encircle our globe.

Using each of my senses in turn, I try to grasp the gravity of this reality. I taste, see, hear, feel, and smell the sin.

Closing

I speak to Christ of whatever surfaces in my mind and heart. I thank him that, in spite of the sinfulness of the world and my share in it, he continues in his mercy to preserve the earth from total destruction.

I close with the Our Father.

Review of Prayer

I write in my journal whatever feelings, such as grief and sense of loss, I experienced during this prayer period.

Section II

The Call of Christ
and Our Response

Week Six, Day 1
Reconciliation . . .
A Time of Forgiveness

JOHN 20:22–23

"Receive the Holy Spirit. If you forgive the sins of any, they are forgiven them; if you retain the sins of any, they are retained."

Commentary

THIS WAS THE EASTER GREETING of Jesus to his gathered and frightened disciples on the day of his resurrection. He came, bringing them the gift of forgiveness.

We must not underestimate this gift. The pagan world knew nothing of forgiveness—only fate. The good news of the Old Testament was that *God forgave* and that, through faith in new beginnings, God acted in the brokenness of his people. In the New Testament, *Jesus forgave* and, in doing so, bore the criticism and the accusation of blasphemy that brought him to his death.

Yet his first words to his disciples were to share with them the incredibly good news that the Spirit of God's own forgiving love dwells within us and that the power to be forgiven and to forgive has been entrusted to us.

Forgiveness awaits us in the heart and hands of the risen Jesus, in the hearts and hands of our fellow Christians. Jesus' words to the disciples invite us to bring the burden of our sinfulness, our brokenness, and our need for forgiveness to another.

"Confess your sins to one another" (James 5:16). For many Christians, this will be a pastor or an ordained minister who is pledged to confidentiality. For those who do not have this as part of their religious tradition, that "other" may be a friend or confidant, some wise man or woman who knows how to listen and how to hear.

After the past weeks of praying about the roots and effects of our sinfulness and God's merciful love for us, we can deepen our healing by making a "confession"—sharing with someone else our need for healing and forgiveness.

The following is a preparation for that confession:*

1. Thanks: What Has Christ Done for Me?

What am I trying to do? How through Christ's help did I succeed? What signs of God's love (people, events) have I experienced in my recent past? Why did things go well? (Was I rested, experiencing less tension, more prayer? Did I have a positive focus?)

2. Examination: Look at the Cross and Ask, "What Have I Done for Christ?

What am I trying to do? How does Christ want me further healed? What were the low points—times of tension, discouragement, boredom, or hurt?

Responses to hurt:

---

*Preparation for confession adapted with permission from *Healing of Memories*, pp. 89–91, 132, by Dennis Linn and Matthew Linn. Copyright © 1974 by the Missionary Society of St. Paul the Apostle in the State of New York. Used by permission of Paulist Press.

Pride—When did I fail to see my true worth? Did I put on a mask for others and so lie, judge, fail to listen, be opinionated or touchy, or ignore the successes of others? What does my critical judging of others say about my own sinfulness? Am I puffed up?

Covetousness—When do I act as if money, possessions, or time are mine rather than a gift?

Lust—How is each part of my body not used to love others?

Anger—What do I fear? Worry about? Resent in others? Find hard to forgive? Have I grown from the failures, tensions, or hurts? When did I react rather than act? When do I avoid difficult persons, such as those who are self-centered, who complain, or who are needy? Do I face my anger or do I deny it, thereby turning it on myself and causing physical symptoms such as headaches or stomach problems?

Gluttony—How do I escape insecurity? Too much drink, food, television watching, study, work, or compulsive spending?

Envy—Do I criticize others to build myself up? Am I bored when others are praised? Do I belittle my success to hear others remind me of it? Do I listen just to the words of others, or do I have empathy with their feelings? Do I make new friends, especially among those who are difficult? Am I faithful to friends? To God?

Laziness—Do I fail to take risks and make sacrifices because I want a tension-free life? Where do I fall into routines rather than live with enthusiasm? Do I learn from the past, live in the present, and plan for the future?

Do I take time to improve myself spiritually, mentally, and physically? What good do I omit doing (corporal and spiritual works)? How do I ignore building up my family, community, church, or those I meet? What parts of my day would Christ live differently?

3. Sorrow: How Did It Hurt Christ in Me or in Others?

Which of the above bothers me the most? How does it hurt Christ in me? In others? How has it spread? Am I sorry just because it hurt me and others or because it hurt Christ too? Am I sorry to the point that I want to change, even if it takes great effort?

4. Healing: Why Am I Doing It for Christ?

Am I feeling or covering my insecurity, guilt, fear, tension, failure, or hostility? Why am I attracted to this action? What do I gain? Power? Popularity? How could I have been hurt that would lead me to respond in that way? Is there any pattern to it? When did it begin? Can I give this all to Christ?

5. Forgiving: Can I Forgive as Christ Forgives?

How has Christ forgiven me (unconditionally, readily, totally)? Can I extend his forgiveness to those who have hurt me? Can I see how they were reacting to other hurts or to my actions and not just to me? Have I forgiven them to the point of seeing some good that came from it, such as having empathy toward those who hurt, trying harder, having more trust in Christ? Do I feel toward them as Christ would? Can I say what Christ would say?

6. Changing: What Will I Do for Christ?

Do I really believe I can be closer to Christ than ever before? Do I feel like the prodigal son (Luke 15:11–32) or the woman who washed Jesus' feet (Luke 7:36–50)? How would Christ live my life? Can I imagine myself doing the same? Why do I want to change?

How can I remind myself to change? How can I exercise my will to change? (See pages 000 and 000.) Would it help me to change if I said a prayer or gave myself a reward when I succeeded? Can I suggest a penance, such as writing a letter, making a visit, giving a compliment, or fasting?

Week Six, Day 2
Tears of Gratitude

···

LUKE 7:36–50

One of the Pharisees asked Jesus to eat with him, and he went into the Pharisee's house and took his place at the table. And a woman in the city, who was a sinner, having learned that he was eating in the Pharisee's house, brought an alabaster jar of ointment. She stood behind him at his feet, weeping, and began to bathe his feet with her tears and to dry them with her hair. Then she continued kissing his feet and anointing them with the ointment. Now when the Pharisee who had invited him saw it, he said to himself, "If this man were a prophet, he would have known who and what kind of woman this is who is touching him—that she is a sinner." Jesus spoke up and said to him, "Simon, I have something to say to you." "Teacher," he replied, "Speak." "A certain creditor had two debtors; one owed five hundred denarii, and the other fifty. When they could not pay, he canceled the debts for both of them. Now which of them will love him more?" Simon answered, "I suppose the one for whom he canceled the greater debt." And Jesus said to him, "You have judged rightly." Then turning toward the woman, he said to Simon, "Do you see this woman? I entered your house; you gave me no water for my feet, but she has bathed my feet with her tears and dried them with her hair. You gave me no kiss, but from the time I came in she has not stopped kissing my feet. You did not anoint my head with oil, but she has anointed my feet with ointment. Therefore, I tell you, her sins, which were many, have been forgiven; hence she has shown great love. But the one to whom little is forgiven, loves little." Then he said to her, "Your sins are forgiven." But those who were at the table with him began to say among themselves, "Who is this who even forgives sins?" And he said to the woman, "Your faith has saved you; go in peace."

Commentary

"PEACE BE WITH YOU!"

"Shalom"—this was the Easter greeting of Jesus (John 20:21). This term, coming to us from the Old Testament, expresses much more than our English word *peace*. It is a wish to someone for their total completeness and well-being, in which nothing is lacking.

This sense of peace is a favored theme in the writings of Luke. In this beautiful story of the woman who washed and anointed the feet of Jesus, St. Luke reveals to us the way to *shalom*. He shows this peace as the fruit of the faith, forgiveness, and love of the woman. In this narration, Luke included a parable of two debtors that serves to interpret the event.

The woman is identified as a sinner. In Aramaic, the language of New Testament times, the word used for sinner was *debtor*. Thus, the parable provides the connecting link between the event and the teaching of Jesus.

The scene opens at the home of the Pharisee. Guests had gathered in the open courtyard where a meal was about to be served. As was the custom, the guests were not seated but reclined on couches near the table.

Jesus was there, having been invited by Simon, a Pharisee. Luke does not tell why Simon invited Jesus. Perhaps he was one of the Pharisees who sincerely admired Jesus, or he may have sought to impress his other guests with the presence of the popular itinerant rabbi. There is also the possibility that he wanted to provoke Jesus into an argument. It was not unusual, when there was a visiting rabbi, for uninvited guests to come and listen to the conversation.

During the meal, from among the onlookers, a woman came forward. She had come deliberately to see Jesus and went directly to the couch, where she "stood behind him at his feet." As she stood there, she began to weep. When her tears fell unintentionally on his feet, she bent over and wiped them with her hair.

Overwhelmed by her emotions, she kissed his feet. She reached for the small vial of perfume that she, like other Jewish women, wore around her neck. Kneeling, she broke open the alabaster jar and proceeded to pour it on his feet, anointing them with its aromatic oil.

Who was this woman? Luke does not tell us precisely. We know only that she had a bad reputation, that she was a "sinner." Although it has been commonly assumed that she was a prostitute, some scholars suggest that she may have been the wife of an outcast, perhaps a despised tax collector (14, p. 138). Simon's inner response to the woman's telling actions was one of irritation. Jesus may have perceived a flash of doubt or skepticism in Simon's eyes.

Jesus spoke: "Simon, I have something to say to you." He began to relate the story of the two debtors who were freed of their indebtedness. Then Jesus posed a question that forced Simon to admit reluctantly the fundamental truth that the more a person is pardoned, the more grateful that person is.

Jesus pressed Simon further. He demonstrated to him how an experience of being unconditionally forgiven can motivate a person to human acts of extraordinary love and generosity. Jesus took Simon's answer to his question and, at the conclusion of the parable, made a direct application to Simon himself. He drew a harsh comparison between Simon and the woman.

Simon had neglected even the most elemental Eastern forms of etiquette. One absolutely never welcomed an invited guest without offering the courtesies of hospitality, which included washing the dust from the traveler's feet, embracing the guest with a kiss, and anointing his or her head with oil.

These outward functional actions had deep inner meanings. For a desert people, water was life, and the kiss was a sign of friendship and forgiveness. Perfumed oil was symbolic of healing and joy. Taken together, these beautiful symbolic acts formed a greeting and an experience of *shalom* for all who entered as guests. Simon had seriously dishonored his guest and his own position as host.

In contrast, the woman came freely and courageously to see Jesus. In his presence her inner gratitude and love for him found expression in her tears. Oblivious to those around her, she spontaneously began to kiss the feet of Jesus repeatedly. Her love spilled over as she poured her fragrant oil on his feet. Jesus called Simon to recognize that such a free and total expression of love could arise only from a heart forgiven and overwhelmed with thankfulness.

Poor Simon! If he showed little love, it was because he had never known the depth of his own thirst and need to be forgiven. To the woman, Jesus said, "Your faith has saved you; go in peace." Who is this man, that he even forgives sins?

Suggested Approach to Prayer

Daily Prayer Pattern
I quiet myself and relax in the presence of God.
I declare my dependence on God.

Grace

I ask Christ our Lord that I may hear his call and be ready and willing to respond with total generosity to his will and intent for me.

Method: Contemplation

I imagine myself as having received the fullness of forgiveness from Christ.

I place myself in the role of the woman and go to the house of the Pharisee.

Using all my senses, I place myself in the situation. I approach Jesus, allowing whatever tears may flow to wash over his feet. I anoint his feet. I look at the face of Jesus and absorb his expression of compassion and love. I listen to and receive his consoling words to me.

Closing

I close my prayer with a conversation with Christ, expressing to him my gratitude and love. I let my heart speak in total openness and surrender. With him I pray the Our Father.

Review of Prayer

I write in my journal any feelings, experiences, or insights I received during this prayer period.

Week Six, Day 3

The Prayer of the Call of Christ and Our Response

Preparation

I begin my prayer by placing myself in the presence of God. Aware of my dependence on him, I beg him to direct everything in me—all I think, do, and say—*more and more* to his praise and service.

I ask for the grace that I may hear his call and be ready and willing to respond with total generosity to his will and intent for me.

Part I

In this first part of my prayer, I bring to mind several men and women who, by their inspiring lives, have won the admiration of countless others. I consider how they have magnetically drawn people to share in their vision and, in some instances, to join them in their work. I consider in some depth the life of a great man or woman. I choose one man or woman I admire—perhaps someone who lived in recent times, such as Pope John XXIII, Mother Teresa, Martin Luther King, or Dorothy Day, or someone from the past, such as Teresa of Ávila or Francis of Assisi. As I bring this person to mind, I reflect on the following:

How have people responded to this person? How have they been inspired to follow the vision and join this person in his or her lifestyle, work, or struggle?

What price has this person paid—all he or she may have given up, such as material possessions, family and home, friends, reputation, or life itself?

Part II

In the second part of my prayer, I see before me Christ our Lord. I prayerfully read the following quotations, considering how Jesus is leader and king:

He has rescued us from the power of darkness and transferred us into the kingdom of his beloved Son, in whom we have redemption, the forgiveness of sins. He is the image of the invisible God, the firstborn of all creation; for in him all things in heaven and on earth were created . . . and in him all things hold together.

COLOSSIANS 1:13–16A, 17B

You are indeed Holy, O Lord, . . .
and you never cease to gather a people to yourself,
so that from the rising of the sun to its setting
a pure sacrifice may be offered to your name.

EUCHARISTIC PRAYER III

For you anointed your Only Begotten Son,
our Lord Jesus Christ, with the oil of gladness

as eternal Priest and King of all creation,

so that, by offering himself on the altar of the Cross

as a spotless sacrifice to bring us peace, . . .

he might present to the immensity of your majesty

an eternal and universal kingdom,

a kingdom of truth and life,

a kingdom of holiness and grace,

a kingdom of justice, love and peace.

PREFACE FROM THE LITURGY OF OUR LORD JESUS CHRIST,

KING OF THE UNIVERSE.

I consider the words of Jesus, our leader, as he says, in effect: "It is my desire to enter into the glory of my Father and to gather the entire world, in unity, to share in this same glory. It is my desire to overcome any evil obstacle that is contrary to that goal. If you wish to join me, you must be willing to labor with me, to do all that is required, and to accept whatever pain or sacrifice is needed, so that together we will enter the fullness of life, the glory of God, my Father."

I consider how, even though Christ is calling the entire world, he is in a particular way calling me to respond and to accept my unique role in the achievement of this goal—the kingdom of God.

I consider how reasonable and sensible this goal is, and how Jesus has assured me of its success. Taking all this into consideration, how can I possibly refuse to join him?

Finally, I consider how people who have totally responded to the call of Jesus have not only offered all they were and had but also withdrawn from and fought against anything that was a hindrance or distraction to their commitment to Jesus.

Closing

I consider what I desire my response and offering to him to be. I speak to Christ of this.

I close with the Our Father.

Review of Prayer

I write in my journal how I am experiencing Christ's care and my response.

Week Six, Day 4

The Call of Paul

PHILIPPIANS 3:7–10

Yet whatever gains I had, these I have come to regard as loss because of Christ. More than that, I regard everything as loss because of the surpassing value of knowing Christ Jesus my Lord. For his sake I have suffered the loss of all things, and I regard them as rubbish, in order that I may gain Christ and be found in him, not having a righteousness of my own that comes from the law, but one that comes through faith in Christ, the righteousness from God based on faith. I want to know Christ and the power of his resurrection and the sharing of his sufferings by becoming like him in his death.

Commentary

ON THE TOAD TO DAMASCUS, Paul passed from death to life.

Paul's conversion was dramatic, a profound rebirth (Acts 9:1–19; 22:6–16; 26:12–18). From that day, he courageously drew on his own transforming experience to inspire others to risk their own passage from darkness to light (Acts 26:17–18).

Paul's conversion was traumatic! At the very moment that his dreams, hopes, and ambitions reached fulfillment, they collapsed. In his blindness, Paul had chosen the wrong road. Gifted and ambitious, Paul allowed the first half of his life to be dictated and controlled by his fanatic allegiance to the Pharisaic value system. This allegiance drove him to channel his energies toward the development and projection of the Pharisaic ideal.

Externally, Paul appeared to be the embodiment of that ideal. Internally, however, he had cut himself off from his own identity and creativity. Through years of study he attained the position of unchallenged expert in the law (Acts 22:3), managing to win the easy approval of the high priests and elders. Having done violence to himself, Paul set out in his misguided zeal to destroy the new Christian disciples.

Paul was undoubtedly headed in the wrong direction. However, "about noon a great light from heaven suddenly shone about" him (Acts 22:6). He heard a voice saying to him, "Saul, Saul, why are you persecuting me?" (22:7). This question set in motion a tremendous upheaval in his life. Overwhelmed by the force and power of such great light, Paul was blinded for three days.

One can imagine the confusion Paul must have experienced! It was as if his entire life had been turned upside down. Filled with questions, he was confronted with a new way of looking at life. In light of this new awareness, his former mind-set was rubbish. All the advantages of his former life were now disadvantages.

Weakened and unable to see, Paul was not left abandoned. God sent a member of the Christian community to minister to him. Into his empty heart Paul received the Spirit of Jesus. With the strength and vision of his risen Lord, Paul saw with new eyes. After a lifetime of seeking God in the law through the pursuit of his own perfection, Paul had met God in the human face of Jesus.

Nothing would ever be the same for Paul. His former self-righteousness and rigid adherence to rules and regulations had given way to an authentic, *right* relationship with the Lord and a commitment to the needs of God's people. The focus had shifted from Paul to Christ, from law to love, from perfection to maturity. Blind obedience yielded to creative vision, intellectual knowledge to the intimate knowing of the heart. The violent persecutor had become the persuasive teacher. All Paul wanted now was to "know Christ and the power of his resurrection and the sharing of his sufferings by becoming like him in his death" (Philippians 3:10).

For Paul, faith could never again be a simple intellectual assent. His faith had become a relationship that put Paul in touch with the fundamental meaning and fullness of life. This extraordinary gift of faith found its expression in Paul's total commitment to Christ. Through this conviction and commitment, Paul received the power of the resurrection, the Spirit of Jesus.

This spirit gave Paul the power to work untiringly in proclaiming the incredible wonder that awaited those who would believe. As poet Gerard Manley Hopkins put it:

As kingfishers catch fire, dragonflies draw flame . . .
Each mortal thing does one thing and the same:
Deals out that being indoors each one dwells;
Selves—goes itself; myself it speaks and spells;
Crying What I do is for me: for that I came.
I say more: the just man justices;
Keeps grace: that keeps all his goings graces;
Acts in God's eye what in God's eye he is—
Christ. (11, p. 95)

For the rest of his life, Paul traveled the known world, suffering every inconvenience and much danger, to deliver the people from darkness to light (Acts 26:18).

Approach to Prayer

I pray the prayer of "The Call of Christ and My Response," pages 170–173, using St. Paul as the person in the first part.

I continue with the second part, Christ's personal call to me, concluding with the closing and review as outlined.

Week Six, Day 5
The Call of Peter

LUKE 5:1–11

Once while Jesus was standing beside the lake of Gennesaret, and the crowd was pressing in on him to hear the word of God, he saw two boats there at the shore of the lake; the fishermen had gone out of them and were washing their nets. He got into one of the boats, the one belonging to Simon, and asked him to put out a little way from the shore. Then he sat down and taught the crowds from the boat. When he had finished speaking, he said to Simon, "Put out into the deep water and let down your nets for a catch." Simon answered, "Master, we have worked all night long but have caught nothing. Yet if you say so, I will let down the nets." When they had done this, they caught so many fish that their nets were beginning to break. So they signaled their partners in the other boat to come and help them. And they came and filled both boats, so that they began to sink. But when Simon Peter saw it, he fell down at Jesus' knees, saying, "Go away from me, Lord, for I am a sinful man!" For he and all who were with him were amazed at the catch of fish that they had taken; and so also were James and John, sons of Zebedee, who were partners with Simon. Then Jesus said to Simon, "Do not be afraid; from now on you will be catching people." When they had brought their boats to shore, they left everything and followed him.

Commentary

THIS IS A STORY ABOUT a miracle, the miracle of a marvelous catch of fish, and the wonder of Peter, who heard the voice of Jesus and "left everything and followed him."

What could be more wonderful than a beautiful catch of fish, especially after a long, hard night of unsuccessful fishing? Luke tells us about this miraculous catch of fish to stir our admiration for Christ and to call forth our belief in him and the treasures he promised us.

Fishing was a way of life for the people who lived along the shores of Gennesaret. Their lives revolved around the daily necessity of catching fish. It was the mainstay of their diet, and fishing was their principal occupation. Fishing was hard work and frequently dangerous, as sudden storms were not uncommon on the lake. Great pride was taken in being an able fisherman, and the skill was handed on from father to son. What could possibly have been more wonderful for these people than to bring home a great catch?

In the New Testament, there are many stories involving fish. One of the most beautiful is the story of how Jesus multiplied and fed bread and fish to the people who were hungry after having spent a day with him in the desert.

Among the stories told of Jesus' appearances after his resurrection is the delightful one in which he ate some fish to show his disciples that he was truly alive (Luke 24:42–43). On another occasion, he surprised his disciples by preparing breakfast for them when they came ashore after a night of fishing. "They saw a charcoal fire there, with fish on it" (John 21:9). Jesus invited them to bring some of their own fish (John 21:9–13).

It follows that, for the early Christians, fish took on significance beyond its primary importance as daily food. The symbolism of the fish is rooted deeply in human history. Long before the time of Jesus, fish held a religious significance. Babylonian writings from the third century b.c. record a myth of Oannes, a fish god, who emerged from the sea to teach men and women the arts and crafts of civilization (46, p. 279). Fish have often symbolized untapped energy and limitless possibilities.

Christ himself came to be symbolized by the fish. In the underground remains of the catacombs of Rome, one can still see the outlines of fish with the Greek acronym for fish—IXØYC—superimposed on it. The letters correspond with the initial Greek letter of each word in the phrase, "Jesus Christ God's Son Saves."

Today we see in the numinous quality of the fish the totality of the risen Christ whose power, when tapped, can release in us miraculous amounts of energy, creativity, and possibilities. This was the promise Christ held out to Peter when he said, "Put out into the deep water and let down your nets for a catch."

A simple, down-to-earth man, Peter had been fishing all his life. Now, at the sight of such a catch and in the presence and power of Jesus, Peter was overwhelmed. He recognized Jesus as Lord! Falling on his knees, he confessed his sinfulness. "Go away from me, Lord, for I am a sinful man!" Jesus reassured him, saying: "Don't be afraid. In companionship with me, you will catch men."

In the power of the word that yielded the miraculous draft of fish, Peter became, in solidarity with Christ, the magnetic lure that would gather many into the kingdom.

Peter continued to be overwhelmed. The power and promise of Christ had gripped him with such force that from then on, he was committed to conforming his life to Christ's. The heart of Peter became the heart of Christ.

He left everything and followed Jesus.

Suggested Approach to Prayer

I pray the prayer of "The Call of Christ and My Response" (pages 170–173), using St. Peter as the person in Part I. I continue with the second part, Christ's personal call to me, concluding with the closing and review as outlined.

Week Six, Day 6

Repetition: My Response

....

I use the prayer, "The Call of Christ and My Response" (pages 170–173). I particularly concentrate on Part II. I write a personal prayer, offering my life to Jesus. During the coming weeks, I will frequently use this prayer.

Appendix:
For Spiritual Directors

The passages and commentaries are keyed to the *Spiritual Exercises of St. Ignatius*. The number in parentheses indicates the numbered paragraph as found in the original text.

For The Principle and Foundation, See Love, Take and Receive series—Love Changes Everything: Romans 5:6–11

Exercise 1: The First, Second, and Third Sin

(50)   The Rebellion of the Angels: 2 Peter 2:1–22

(51)   Sin of Adam and Eve

        The Choice: Living for Ourselves or for God:
        Genesis 3:1–7 .

        The Ratification of Sin: Romans 5:12–21

(52)   The Person in Hell

        One Person's Fall: Luke 16:19–31

Exercise 2: The Consequences of Sin

(56)   A Warning from History: Ezekiel 16:1–22, 59–63

        Remembering, Parts 1 and 2: Ezekiel 16:1–22,
        59–63

(57)   You Are the One: 2 Samuel 11:1–21, 27; 12:1, 7–10,
        13–25

(58)   Out of the Depths: Psalm 130

(59)   God Is God: Job 42:1–6

(60)   Homelessness: Ezekiel 36:25–29

        A Cry for Mercy: Psalm 51

Exercise 3: The Roots of Personal Sinfulness

(63)   Decision to Love: Matthew 25:31–46

The Struggle: Romans 7:14–25

You Must Choose!: 1 John 2:12–17

Seduction: James 1:13–18

Blessing or Curse?: James 3:2–12

Self-Encounter: James 4:1–10

False Treasure: Luke 12:16–21

The Masks of Hypocrisy: Mark 7:1–23

Pharisee of Tax Collector?: Luke 18:9–14

Exercise 4: God's Merciful Forgiveness

(64)   The Forgiving Father: Luke 15:11–32

Coming Home: Luke 15:11–32

Exercise 5: Meditation on Hell

(65)   The Final Loss, Parts 1 and 2: Hebrews 10:26–29

The Ultimate Collapse: Revelations 18:2, 21–23

Christ the King and His Call

(90)   Reconciliation . . . A Time of Forgiveness: John
20:22–23

(91–98) Tears of Gratitude: Luke 7:36–50

The Prayer of the Call of Christ and Our Response

The Call of Paul: Philippians 3:7–10

The Call of Peter: Luke 5:1–11

(98)   Repetition: My Response

Bibliography

1. Abbot, Walter M., ed. *The Documents of Vatican II*. New York: American Press, 1966.

2. Albright, W. F., and C. S. Mann. *Matthew*. Garden City, NY: Doubleday & Co., 1971.

3. Anderson, Bernard W. *Understanding the Old Testament*. Englewood Cliffs, NJ: Prentice-Hall, 1975.

4. Barclay, William. *The Daily Study Bible Series*. Philadelphia: Westminster Press, 1975.

5. Barth, Karl. *A Shorter Commentary on Romans*. Richmond, VA: John Knox Press, 1963.

6. Barth, Markus. *Ephesians 1–3*. Garden City, NY: Doubleday & Co., 1974.

7. Bergant, Diane. *Job, Ecclesiastes*. Wilmington, DE: Michael Glazier, 1982.

8. Blenkinsopp, Joseph. *From Adam to Abraham*. Glen Rock, NJ: Paulist Press, 1966.

9. Boadt, Lawrence. *Jeremiah 1–25*. Wilmington, DE: Michael Glazier, 1982.

10. Boucher, Madeleine I. *The Parables*. Wilmington, DE: Michael Glazier, 1981.

11. Bridges, Robert, ed. *Poems of Gerard Manley Hopkins*. New York: Oxford University Press, 1948.

12. Bright, John. *Jeremiah*. Garden City, NY: Doubleday & Co., 1965.

13. Brown, Raymond. *The Epistles of John*. Garden City, NY: Doubleday & Co., 1982.

14. Brown, Raymond, et al. *The Jerome Biblical Commentary*. Englewood Cliffs, NJ: Prentice-Hall, 1968.

15. Buchanan, George Wesley. *To the Hebrews*. Garden City, NY: Doubleday & Co., 1972.

16. Caird, G. B. *Saint Luke*. London: Penguin Books, 1963.

17. Casey, Juliana. *Hebrews*. Wilmington, DE: Michael Glazier, 1980.

18. Conroy, Charles. *1–2 Samuel, 1–2 Kings*. Wilmington, DE: Michael Glazier, 1980.

19. Cowan, Marian, C.S.J., and John C. Futrell, S.J. *The Spiritual Exercises of St. Ignatius of Loyola: A Handbook for Directors*. New York: Le Jacq Publishing, 1982.

20. Dahood, Mitchell. *Psalms II, III.* Garden City, NY: Doubleday & Co., 1968, 1970.

21. de Mello, Anthony, S.J. *Sadhana, A Way to God.* St. Louis: Institute of Jesuit Sources, 1978.

22. Dodd, C. H. *The Parables of the Kingdom.* New York: Charles Scribner & Sons, 1961.

23. English, John, S.J. *Spiritual Freedom.* Guelph, ON: Loyola House, 1974.

24. Erickson, Erik. *Childhood and Society.* New York: W. W. Norton and Co., 1963.

25. Fenton, J. C. *Saint Matthew.* Baltimore: Penguin Books, 1963.

26. Ferrucci, Piero. *What We May Be.* Los Angeles: J. P. Tarcher, 1982.

27. Fitzmeyer, Joseph. *The Gospel According to Luke I–IX.* Garden City, NY: Doubleday & Co., 1981.

28. Fleming, S. J. *The Spiritual Exercises of St. Ignatius: A Literal Translation and a Contemporary Reading.* St. Louis: Institute of Jesuit Sources, 1978.

29. Ford, J. Massyngberde. *Revelations.* Garden City, NY: Doubleday & Co., 1975.

30. Fox, Matthew. *Breakthrough*. Garden City, NY: Image Books, 1977.

31. Getty, Mary Ann. *Philippians and Philemon*. Wilmington, DE: Michael Glazier, 1980.

32. Gill, Jean. *Images of My Self.* New York: Paulist Press, 1982.

33. Greenberg, Mosche. *Ezechiel, 1–20*. Garden City, NY: Doubleday & Co., 1983.

34. Hanson, James H. *Making Contact: Prayer in the Name of Jesus*. Minneapolis: Augsberg Publishing House, 1978.

35. Harrington, Wilfred. *Mark*. Wilmington, DE: Michael Glazier, 1979.

36. Heschel, Abraham J. *The Prophets*. New York: Harper and Row, 1962.

37. Hitter, Joseph. "The First Week and the Love of God." *The Way*, supplement 34 (autumn 1978): 26–34.

38. Hughes, Gerard W. "The First Week and the Formation of Conscience." *The Way*, supplement 24 (spring 1978): 6–14.

39. Jung, Carl G. *Man and His Symbols*. New York: Valor Publications, 1964.

40. Kugelman, Richard. *James and Jude*. Wilmington, DE: Michael Glazier, 1980.

41. Kung, Hans. *On Being a Christian*. Garden City, NY: Doubleday & Co., 1976.

42. La Verdiere, Eugene. *Luke*. Wilmington, DE: Michael Glazier, 1980.

43. Leslie, Elmer A. *The Psalms*. New York: Abingdon Press, 1949.

44. Linn, Matthew, and Dennis Linn. *Healing of Memories*. New York: Paulist Press, 1974.

45. McBrien, Richard. *Catholicism. 2 vols*. Minneapolis: Winston Press, 1980.

46. McKenzie, John. *Dictionary of the Bible*. Milwaukee, WI: Bruce Publishing Co., 1965.

47. McPalin, James. *John*. Wilmington, DE: Michael Glazier, 1979.

48. Magana, Jose, S.J. *A Strategy for Liberation*. Hicksville, NY: Exposition Press, 1974.

49. Maher, Michael. *Genesis*. Wilmington, DE: Michael Glazier, 1982.

50. Meier, John P. *Matthew*. Wilmington, DE: Michael Glazier, 1980.

51. Menninger, Karl. *Whatever Became of Sin?* New York: Hawthorn Books, 1973.

52. Miller, William A. Make *Friends with Your Shadow*. Minneapolis: Augsburg Publishing Co., 1981.

53. Mische, Patricia. "A New Genesis in Religious Communities and World Community." *Sisters Today 53*, no. 7 (March 1982): 387–398.

54. Ninehan, D. E. *Mark*. Baltimore: Penguin Books, 1963.

55. Osick, Carolyn. "The First Week of the Spiritual Exercises and the Conversion of St. Paul." *Review for Religious 36*, no. 5 (September 1977): 657–665.

56. Pennington, M. Basil. *Centering Prayer*. Garden City, NY: Image Books, 1982.

57. Perkins, Pheme. *The Johannine Epistles*. Wilmington, DE: Michael Glazier, 1979.

58. Pope, Marvin H. *Job*. Garden City, NY: Doubleday & Co., 1965.

59. Rahner, Karl. *Spiritual Exercises*. New York: Herder and Herder, 1956.

60. Reicke, B. *The Epistles of James, Peter and Jude*. Garden City, NY: Doubleday & Co., 1964.

61. Rollings, Wayne G. *Jung and the Bible*. Atlanta: John Knox Press, 1983.

62. Sanford, John A. *The Kingdom Within*. New York: Paulist Press, 1970.

63. Sanford, John A. *The Shadow Side of Reality*. New York: Crossroad Publishing Co., 1981.

64. Senior, Donald. *1 & 2 Peter*. Wilmington, DE: Michael Glazier, 1980.

65. Shakespeare, William. *The Complete Works of Wm. Shakespeare. Vol. 2*. Garden City, NY: Nelson Doubleday, n.d.

66. Speiser, E. A. *Genesis*. Garden City, NY: Doubleday & Co., 1964.

67. Stanley, David M. *A Modern Spiritual Approach to the Spiritual Exercises*. St. Louis: Institute of Jesuit Sources, 1971.

68. Stuhmueller, Carroll. *Psalm 1, Psalm 2*. Wilmington, DE: Michael Glazier, 1983.

69. Swain, Lionel. *Ephesians*. Wilmington, DE: Michael Glazier, 1980.

70. Taylor, Vincent. *The Gospel according to St. Mark*. New York: St. Martin's Press, 1966.

71. Teilhard de Chardin, Pierre. *The Divine Milieu*. New York: Harper and Row, Publisher, 1960.

72. Veltri, John, S.J. *Orientations: Vol. 1. A Collection of Helps for Prayer.* Guelph, ON: Loyola House, 1979.

73. Veltri, John, S.J. *Orientations: Vol. II. Annotation 19: Tentative Edition.* Guelph, ON: Loyola House, 1981.

74. Woodman, Marion. *Addiction to Perfection.* Toronto: Inner City Books, 1982.

About the Authors

....

JACQUELINE SYRUP BERGAN, A WIFE, mother, and grandmother, likes to say that she went from putting people to sleep as a nurse anesthetist to waking them up through her ministry of retreat work and spiritual direction. She and her husband, Leonard, live in Wisconsin during the summer and spend the remainder of their time in Arizona, where Jacqueline offers spiritual direction through the Franciscan Center in Scottsdale and teaches Ignatian spirituality at the Arizona Ecumenical Institute for Spiritual Direction.

Marie Schwan is a Sister of St. Joseph, currently in ministry in the diocese of Rapid City, South Dakota, where she facilitates classes in the Commissioned Lay Ministry Program and the Diaconate Formation program and offers spiritual direction. A teacher by profession, she has served in administration and formation in her congregation, and she spent fourteen years as associate director of Jesuit Retreat House in Oshkosh, Wisconsin. Also by Jacqueline Syrup Bergan and Marie Schwan, CSJ:

Also Available

RETREAT IN THE REAL WORLD
ANDY ALEXANDER, SJ
MAUREEN McCANN WALDON
LARRY GILLICK, SJ

$14.95 • PB • 2913-8

What do you imagine when someone mentions the word "retreat"? Your mind may conjure images of withdrawing from life and traveling to a distant retreat house away from home. But who has time for that? What if you didn't have to go to a retreat to enjoy its many benefits . . . what if the retreat came to you?

Retreat in the Real World offers the unique opportunity to create an in-depth, self-directed Ignatian retreat on your own time. This 34-week retreat can be started at any point in the calendar year and can be experienced anywhere that works for you. You can even experience the retreat by yourself or in conjunction with others.

Also Available

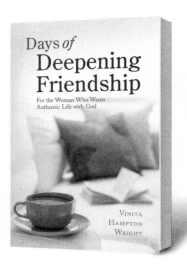

**DAYS OF DEEPENING
FRIENDSHIP**

VINITA HAMPTON WRIGHT

$13.95 • PB • 2811-7

Acclaimed author and speaker Vinita Hampton Wright invites women to embark upon a dynamic friendship with God that is both stunning in its wisdom and delightful in its daily unfolding. Using Scripture, meditations, stories, and written exercises, *Days of Deepening Friendship* encourages women to radically rethink their approach to God and to explore the deeper regions of this very special relationship.

Wright taps the proven wisdom of Ignatian spirituality by employing prayer, imagination, action, and reflection, making *Days of Deepening Friendship* an ideal spiritual workshop for women looking to be free to be themselves and to express themselves—without fear—to God.

Continue your Ignatian spirituality journey online . . .

Learn more about prayer, spiritual direction,
retreats, and how to make good decisions at

www.ignatianspirituality.com